Bohemia

Sweden

Jerusalem

Tripoli

Russia

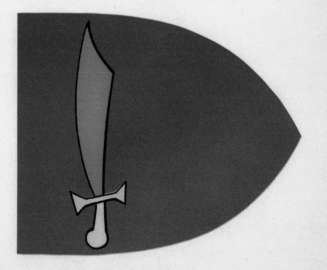

Transylvania

That Are in the World," the first book about flags, written in the fourteenth century.

Flags
of All Nations
And The People
Who Live Under Them

By Mary Elting and Franklin Folsom

**in consultation with
the Flag Research Center
and Edwin M. Moser**

Library of Congress Catalog Card Number: 67-23799

Grosset & Dunlap • New York

CONTENTS

Acknowledgments

This book was made possible because the various countries, directly or through their embassies in Washington, D.C., or their Permanent Missions to the United Nations, graciously answered many questions and supplied useful materials. Additional help came from the Office of Public Information of the United Nations; from the Geographer of the Bureau of Intelligence and Research, Department of State, Washington, D.C., and from the American Geographic Society. To all of them go our thanks. For help with special problems we are indebted to the Information Division of the New York Public Library; Jean R. Longland, Curator, the Library of the Hispanic Society; Douglas C. Ewing, Assistant Curator, the Pierpont Morgan Library; L. McKimmie, Editorial Department, Frederick Warne and Co., Ltd., London; Whitney Smith, Director of the Flag Research Center. In preparing and checking our material, we also consulted *The Flag Book of the United Nations* (1963); *The United Nations Demographic Yearbook; Flags of the World,* edited by E. M. C. Barraclough (1965); *The Book of Flags* by Gordon Campbell and I. O. Evans; *The Flag Bulletin,* Vols. I-VII:2, published by Flag Research Center, 17 Farmcrest Ave., Lexington, Mass.; *Annin Banner;* and the special flag numbers of the *National Geographic Magazine:* October, 1917; September, 1934; May, 1949; and February, 1951. Special thanks go also to Archie Bennett for his art direction, layout and design, and to E. M. Moser, Fairleigh Dickinson University, whose assistance with historical research and creative participation helped shape this book.

Mary Elting and Franklin Folsom

Picture Credits

Austrian Information Service (O. V. W. Hubmann), 24; Casa de Portugal, N. Y., 114; *China Pictorial,* 41; Consulate General of New Zealand, N. Y., 104; Irish International Airlines (John Reader), 73; Luxembourg Consulate General, N. Y. (Tony Krier), 90; Romanian Permanent Mission to the United Nations, 116; Swedish Information Service, 128; Swiss National Tourist Office, 129; Turkish Information Office, 137; UNESCO, 36, 42, 60 (S. Reiske), 61 (left, Marc and Evelyne Bernheim), 70, 76 (top, Eric Schwab, bottom, Paul Almasy), 78 (from *Unesco Courier,* courtesy Japanese Embassy, Paris), 80 (P. A. Pittet), 88, 94 (P. A. Pittet), 96 (Paul Almasy), 100 (Gerda Bohm), 101 (Francis Brunel), 105 (Studio Raccah), 106 (Almasy-Vauthey), 108 (Christopher Hills), 112 (Bonos), 113 (Centralna Ageneja Fotograficzna, Warszawa), 132 (Garroud), 140 (Marc Riboud), 150 (Walter Gerull); United Nations, 17, 28, 29, 32, 33, 34, 37, 40, 45, 48 (right), 49, 52, 53, 54, 56, 57, 61 (right), 62 (bottom), 64, 65, 69, 72, 85, 89, 92, 126, 133, 141, 153; Wide World Photos, 21, 24, 26, 30, 46, 48 (left), 62 (top), 82, 84, 110, 121, 122, 144, 148. All flags in color by Harry McChesney.

Totem Pole

Roman Standard

Egyptian Standard

How Flags Began

ALL PEOPLE use symbols. We talk, uttering sounds to represent things or actions or emotions or ideas. If we write, we use lines and curves and dots to stand for sounds. We dress in certain ways and not in others. The clothes we wear are symbols, showing that we are male or female, priest or soldier, nurse or nun.

The history of any kind of symbol can usually reveal something interesting and important about people who have used it. Certainly this is true of those colorful emblems of nationhood called flags.

The story of flags begins in prehistoric times, long before cloth had even been invented. In those days, men were hunters, and they felt very close to the whole animal world. They drew pictures of animals and carved them in wood or stone. Perhaps some people thought that they got magic help from one particular creature. They may even have believed that a distant ancestor of theirs was a bear, a coyote or an eagle. At any rate, groups of people who were relatives (they are called clans) often adopted the name of an animal or bird or fish, and it then became a clan symbol. The word for this clan symbol, in the language of one American Indian tribe, was *totem*. Now all such symbols are called totems.

8

Carvings of totems were sometimes placed over doors or on poles in front of houses. Warriors carried their totems into battle. The animal or bird was often painted on their shields, or its image might be carried on a long stick called a standard. This custom proved useful. When soldiers were scattered during a fight, they could rejoin their fellows by looking for the standard that belonged to their leader.

Totems and Standards

In Egypt, more than five thousand years ago, a falcon was the totem of the king, who was known as the pharaoh. People believed, in fact, that the pharaoh actually was a falcon hatched from an egg, and for a very long time this bird remained the symbol of Egyptian rulers. When soldiers of the first pharaoh marched, they carried standards with images of falcons on top. (Just such a scene has been found carved in stone.) Later pharaohs, instead of putting the whole bird on the standard, sometimes displayed only a few of its feathers. As time went on, little cloth streamers were sometimes added beneath the feathers, but if these had any special meaning, people have forgotten what it was. The cloth strips may have been nothing but decorations to attract attention.

Whether or not this custom began in Egypt, totems appeared on battlefields in many places. Soldiers of ancient Assyria rallied around a disc that was held aloft. Painted on it was the figure of a bull, or two bulls tied together by their tails. Greek armies followed similar totems—an owl for the city of Athens, a winged horse for Corinth, a bull for Boeotia. One fast-moving army had a slow-moving tortoise on its standard.

In the earliest days of Rome, every small group of soldiers carried a pole with a bundle of hay on top. That was their standard. Later armies used animal figures as the Greeks did, and there were five such standards in service for a long time. Then a Roman leader did away with all except one—an eagle, which came to be a symbol for military power in many parts of the world. Still later, a Roman military unit sometimes carried a square piece of decorated cloth hanging from a crossbar that was itself suspended from a pole.

A different kind of symbol is said to have appeared in 80 B.C. when the Persians revolted against a particularly despotic ruler. The leader of the rebels was a blacksmith, and, according to legend, his work-apron was raised as a standard above the fighting. Very much later, in the sixteenth century, when German peasants revolted against feudal lords, they used a picture of a peasant's shoe on their flag. But this is getting ahead of the story.

9

The First Real Flags

In ancient times, the fashion of dressing up a totem with a streamer appeared in other lands besides Egypt. Some armies began to use streamers alone on standards, and this idea seems to have spread eastward, perhaps through India, until it reached China, where the first real flags were flown. About 1100 B.C., a Chinese royal family had a flag made of white cloth attached to a pole. Much later, Chinese pictures showed cavalrymen carrying rectangular flags with recognizable patterns on them. Some were attached at the top to a crossbar hung from a pole in the manner of the Roman banners; others were fastened at the side, as flags are today.

A triangular shape, also fastened at the side, became the favorite in India, and a flag made of two triangles still flies in Nepal, a country on the Indian border (see NEPAL).

Moslem Colors

From India and China, flags spread westward, just as streamers may once have spread to the east. Arabia had them at least by the seventh century A.D., when an Arab named Mohammed founded a new religion which came to be called Islam, meaning "submission to God's will." Islam soon inspired armies to burst out of Arabia, waging what the faithful called Holy Wars to convert unbelievers. Mohammed himself was said to have used a black flag in his military campaigns. According to tradition, the black Flag of the Prophet was really the curtain that hung at the entrance to the tent of Mohammed's favorite wife. Many Moslems (followers of Islam) believe that this original flag still exists somewhere in the world today.

After Mohammed died in A.D. 632, new leaders known as *caliphs* took his place, and the colors of their flags depended on what family they belonged to. Those in the Omayyad family had a white one, possibly because Mohammed was supposed to have worn a white turban. The Abbassid family used black, as the Prophet himself had done. The Fatimid caliphs' flag was green because Mohammed was supposed to have worn a green coat. Ever since the days of those early caliphs, green, white and black have remained traditional colors in the Moslem world.

One group of Moslems, known as the Kharijites, had strong disagreements with the caliphs, and they chose a red flag. In places where their descendants live—for example, along the eastern coast of Arabia —the red flag is still flown to this day.

Arab armies, waging their Holy Wars, swept over Western and Central Asia, conquered all of North Africa, and moved up into Europe, subduing Spain. Wherever they went, they carried their flags with them. In time, Christian armies counterattacked the energetic Arabs. Men

Soldiers in Spain carrying flags. (From an early thirteenth century manuscript in the Pierpont Morgan Library, New York.)

known as Crusaders marched into Palestine to take and hold for a while the sacred places of the Christian religion.

When armies from Western Europe set off for Palestine, the Roman Catholic Pope ordered all Christians along the way to give them help, and it was suggested that a Crusader could identify himself clearly by displaying a cross. (The word *crusade* comes from the Spanish word *cruz,* meaning cross.) In practice, this meant putting crosses on shields or on the cloth coverings men wore over armor to keep the metal from getting uncomfortably hot in the sun. These coverings were called surcoats or *coats of arms.*

Signatures for Illiterates

By the time of the Third Crusade, late in the twelfth century, there were Christian soldiers in Palestine from many parts of Europe, all wearing helmets, armor and coats that looked very much alike. Often it was hard to tell who was who, so to solve the problem, some men put identification marks around the crosses on their coats and shields. Since a cross divides an area into four sections, emblems could be placed in all four spaces. Each man invented a design for his own emblem, which then served as a kind of signature that could be recognized at a distance, even by those who could not read — and most Crusaders did not know their ABC's.

In time, the designs on the cloth were themselves called coats of arms. Finally, the name came to mean simply the design, even when it was not a coat at all. A coat of arms was also called *armorial bearings,* or simply *arms.* These emblems first appeared only on coats, shields and coverings for horses; later they turned up in many other places as well — on buttons, on ladies' dresses, as wall decorations. In some ways they served the same purpose as today's trademarks and cattle brands.

A man's armorial bearings often suggested a story of some kind, just as clan totems once did. The design might tell about his castle, about animals he liked to hunt, or monsters he hoped would bring him luck and frighten his foes. It might include birds and flowers, lions he had never seen, or dragons he was sure existed somewhere. A man who had an identification of this sort passed it along to his eldest son when he died, and in this way coats of arms became part of family property. Powerful families all had them; ambitious families all wanted them.

Learning from Moslems

In Palestine, the Christians learned many things from the Moslems they had come to fight: to eat new foods and dress in new fabrics (though not, according to Arab writers, to take baths as Moslems did). They discovered new ways of building castles and churches, and they took a fancy to the Moslem custom of carrying flags.

After the Crusaders returned to Western Europe, flags suddenly became more popular there. A few were already in use, but now there was a sort of flag explosion. Flags flew at the tips of armed men's lances, on the masts of ships, over castles and cities. In the tiny kingdoms and principalities that dotted Europe, ruling families began to use their own personal flags. Many of these have been preserved in an illustrated book written by a certain Spanish friar in the middle of the fourteenth century. His title, *Book of the Knowledge of All the Kingdoms, Lords and Lordships That Are in the World,* was somewhat exaggerated, but he did travel prodigiously, gathering information and sketching flags, some of which appear on pages 14 and 15.

Fairly simple designs were used on most of the flags collected by the friar (whose name we do not know), but the making of armorial bearings for princes and noblemen gradually became more complicated. A man often inherited or acquired the right to use two or more of these emblems, and he had to crowd them into a rather small space. And, of course, everyone wanted to be sure *his* design was different from others. Experts were needed to solve these problems and to design new arms which rulers could give to their subjects as rewards.

It so happened that princes in the Middle Ages already had in their courts officials (called *heralds*) who had become familiar with coats of arms. In those days a favorite sporting event was a mock battle between armored men on horseback who charged across a field with long lances, each one trying to force his opponent out of the saddle. The mock fighting was called *jousting,* and the whole colorful gathering of knights and noblemen was a *tourney* or *tournament,* attracting large numbers of competitors concealed inside their armor. The heralds who arranged the contests had to be able to recognize each man by looking at his coat of arms.

After tournaments went out of fashion, the use of armorial bearings continued, and so did the need for special knowledge about them. The heralds, who had once simply identified coats of arms, began to design them. Since each design had to be unique and easily distinguishable from others, heralds began to cooperate in their work—even when their employers were hostile to one another. In time of war, heralds were considered neutral and could pass freely between enemy camps.

As they came to share knowledge, heralds developed *heraldry*—rules for describing and designing coats of arms, as well as a set of technical terms internationally used. Much of their special language was based on a French dialect spoken by Normans. For example, the heralds' word for red was *gules* (pronounced GOOLZ), a Norman name for a fur neckpiece that had been dyed red. Gold and silver—or yellow and white—were called *metals,* and it was considered against the rules of heraldry to design a coat of arms that had metal touching metal. In other words, gold and silver must never be placed next to each other, but must have some

France

Germany

Granada

Frisia

other color in between; and colors were always to be separated by a metal. A *supporter* was a figure—a horse or a lion, for example—which a nobleman might be allowed to display on one side or on both sides of a shield in his coat of arms.

In the beginning, a coat of arms was the personal emblem of a military man. Then families, kingdoms, cities, states and nations all had arms. Today, when a country becomes independent, it often adopts a coat of arms, as well as a new flag.

Late in the Middle Ages, a set of rules developed for flags. Each nobleman had a flag of his own, and in England, its size depended on his rank. An emperor's flag was six feet square; a king's flag was five feet square; and so on, down through dukes, earls and others, to the knights who could only carry triangular pennants.

Until about the fifteenth century, most flags still belonged to individuals who ruled and were known in a limited area. Then modern nations began to develop, as small kingdoms and principalities joined or conquered one another. Armies and fleets grew larger; soldiers began to serve not princelings who owned small parts of the land, but monarchs who directed the affairs of large countries. More and more, flags came to stand for nations, rather than just individuals or families.

As time passed, heralds became less important, but they did not disappear altogether. In England and Scotland today, heralds still keep track of old coats of arms, design new ones, and are in charge of certain official ceremonies.

The Red Flag of Defiance

Although most countries no longer have heralds, flag lore and customs continue. There is, for example, a long tradition behind the use of red flags.

In very early times, red seems to have stood for bravery, aggressiveness or defiance. Perhaps the origin of this meaning is simple: blood is shed in battle, and blood is red. At any rate, a red flag in Roman times was a symbol of combat; by raising a red standard or flag above his tent, a Roman general told his troops to prepare for battle. Roman armies once dominated much of Europe, and they left many of their customs behind. Possibly that is why Frenchmen of Normandy raised red streamers on their vessels in the thirteenth century when they were about to engage in combat with ships from England.

Much earlier, the rebel Kharijite sect had adopted a red flag and used it in a struggle with other Moslem groups. In the end they were pushed to the fringes of the Moslem world, along the uninviting coast of the Arabian Peninsula, where, partly from necessity, many of them took to piracy. Flying a red flag, they preyed on foreign vessels in the Persian Gulf.

Very likely, the red flag of these pirates was known to seamen who sailed into the Persian Gulf from other parts of the world. Certainly, in the seventeenth and eighteenth centuries, red was the pirate color in common use on the high seas. By 1790, a book about flags listed a red one as "the flag of defiance."

Java

In France at that time, a red flag also had a special military use: if the government declared an emergency, it raised a red flag as a sign that peacetime laws were suspended and that the armed forces had taken over control. In other words, the red flag was a symbol of martial law. Although the French revolution had begun in 1789, King Louis XVI was still allowed to remain on the throne because he had given up some of his power and had promised to rule under a constitution. Secretly, however, Louis was plotting to overthrow the constitutional government and recover absolute power. When the plot was discovered, many people thought the time had come to rid themselves of the king entirely. Thousands came to a great rally to sign a petition for the formation of a republic. The government regarded this as an emergency, hoisted the red flag and declared martial law. Soon afterward the National Guard fired on the petitioners, killing many of them.

Toulouse

Now the republicans developed the ingenious idea that it was the king who was in revolt against the people — and that a serious emergency had indeed developed. Why not declare martial law against the king and his supporters? A red flag was raised, and before long, the revolutionists succeeded in establishing a republic.

Russia

No one knows who had this idea. Perhaps it came from a sailor or a scholar who knew that a red flag often served as a flag of defiance. At any rate, it became a symbol of revolution from then on. Communists used it in another French revolution in 1871. Socialists adopted it, and it became the flag of the British Labour Party. In several countries communists used it after World War I and again after World War II. When revolutionists succeeded in Russia and China, the old red flag, with other symbols added, was adopted by the new governments.

Jerusalem

Flag Vocabulary

Similar stories about flags—or about elements of flag design—appear later on in this book, where flags of specific countries are described. Some of the terms used in descriptions are those which come from the special study of flags, sometimes called *vexillology*. Here are a few of the technical words that need explanation:

A flag can be divided into four quarters. The one in the upper left, next to the flagpole, is the most important and is called the *canton*. In it special emblems may appear—for example, the sun of Uruguay, the hammer-and-sickle and star of the Soviet Union, the fifty stars of the United States. The background against which these emblems are set is called the *field*. Thus, the stars of the United States flag appear in a blue field. The word *field* can also be used to describe any part of a flag on which emblems or designs are placed. The emblems themselves are called *charges,* and we say that the British Union Flag is *charged* with three crosses on a blue field. The flag of Laos is charged with a white three-headed elephant (among other things).

The part of the flag nearest the flagpole is the *hoist*. The part farthest away is the *fly*.

Banner and *standard* are really synonyms for flag, although each can have a special meaning. *Colors* is a word used for military flags.

A *national flag* is exactly what it sounds like — a flag for the whole country, not one to be used only by a ruler or president or an army or navy. In most countries, ordinary citizens are permitted to fly it, and it represents the country elsewhere in the world. The United States flag and the French Tricolor are national flags. Some countries have *state* or *government flags* in addition to the national flags. Special emblems often appear on these, and they are flown from government buildings.

There is not room in this book for every kind of flag. In the pages that follow, all the independent countries in the world are represented, as well as a few of the countries that are partly independent. The flags shown and discussed here are national flags, with a few exceptions which are noted in each case in the text. Under each flag are numerals that give its proper proportions. For example, 2:3 means that the height is two-thirds of the length.

Flags for Man-Made Countries and Outer Space

NEW ATLANTIS: Six miles from Jamaica, in the Caribbean Sea, a raft twelve feet long and six feet wide rides at anchor above a sandbar. The owner of this raft declared, on July 4, 1964, that it was an independent country called New Atlantis, with a flag of its own. The blue field of the flag represents the ocean on which New Atlantis floats; a globe inside a triangle in the center of the field represents the study of all the world's oceans. According to the raft's owner, Leicester Hemingway, who calls himself President of New Atlantis, his "country" is to be devoted to the science of oceanography, and in time the raft will be converted into a platform resting on the sandbar. Seven people claim to be citizens of New Atlantis, which may be the first of many man-made countries built up outside the boundaries of any existing state.

MOON: The first space flag reached the moon on February 23, 1966. It was made of metal, in the triangular shape of a pennant. On one side of the flag, designs representing the Earth and Moon were connected by a line to show the route traveled by Luna IX, the Russian spacecraft which carried it. On the other side was the Soviet coat of arms and *Union of Soviet Socialist Republics,* written in Cyrillic letters.

Afghans inspect an exhibit of handicrafts at the festival held on their national independence day.

AFGHANISTAN (af-GAN-is-tan): In 1929, the king of Afghanistan ordered a new flag which has remained in use ever since. The previous flag had been black, with a white coat of arms. The new one, although less somber, still has a black stripe that stands for the country's hard, dark past. A red stripe is for wars fought against aggressors — and there have been many of them since very ancient times. The green stands for freedom and prosperity. In the center of the coat of arms a Moslem mosque shows that Islam is the official religion. The number 1348 gives the date, according to the Moslem calendar, which corresponds to 1929 on the Western (Gregorian) calendar. At the bottom, the name Afghanistan appears in Arabic script.

The wreath of wheat in the coat of arms suggests that this is a country of farmers. It also reminds people how one branch of the royal family had its beginnings in 1747. That year, after the ruler of the Afghan Empire was assassinated, a tribal council met to discuss future plans. While the leaders talked, a dervish (Moslem holy man) appeared, carrying a wreath of wheat which he put on the head of a certain army officer. This man, the council decided, should be the new king.

Afghanistan was a large empire in the eighteenth century, then lost much of its territory to the British Empire. In 1919, the country won its independence from Britain, and the present monarchy began in 1929.

The majority of the 16,000,000 Afghans belong to the Pakhtun, or Pathan, tribes. Others are Tajiks, Hazaras, Turkmans and Uzbeks. More than half the people speak Pashtu, but Dari is the official government language. Both Pashtu and Dari are taught in the schools. The country's official name is the Kingdom of Afghanistan. *Member, United Nations.*

ALBANIA (al-BANE-ee-yuh): The Albanians' name for their country is Shqiperia, which means "Land of the Eagle." They call themselves "Children of the Eagle," partly because the great bird does live in their country's high mountains and partly because an old legend says the eagle was their first ancestor.

Albanians are really descendants of an ancient people known as Illyrians who once ruled a large part of southeastern Europe and sailed their pirate ships all over the Mediterranean Sea. In the third century B.C., Illyria became part of the Roman Empire. The Romans had great respect for the skilled Illyrian soldiers, who often fought with slingshots, and for Illyrian generals, several of whom became emperors of Rome. One was Constantine the Great, who gave religious freedom to Christians.

After the end of the Roman Empire, the Illyrian language gradually changed and became modern Albanian. The country itself remained poor and backward as it fought against one foreign invader after another. In 1443, an Albanian patriot, George Kastrioti, led his people in a revolt against their latest conquerors, the Turks. Kastrioti had once served in the Turkish army and had been given the name Iskander Bey, meaning Sir Alexander. Since the Turkish words were hard for the Albanians to pronounce, they called him Skanderbeg. They still do, to this day.

For more than twenty years the Turks sent their largest and best armies against Skanderbeg. He defeated them all. Then he died of fever, and by 1501 the Turks had reconquered the country. When they ordered all Christians to become Moslems, thousands fled to Italy, where their descendants still live in their own villages, speaking both Albanian and Italian. Albania won freedom from Turkey in 1912, was invaded by Italy in 1939, and in 1944 became independent again. This time it had a government headed by communists.

The Albanian flag has a two-headed black eagle on a red background. This was the flag Skanderbeg used in his revolt against the Turks, and it is very dear to Albanians — both because of its history and because they are "Children of the Eagle." A gold-edged red star, a symbol of communism, was added in 1944.

Most of the 1,700,000 Albanians were born into the Moslem faith, about one-fifth into the Eastern Orthodox Church, and one-seventh into the Roman Catholic Church. Many do not now practice any religion. The official name of their country is the People's Republic of Albania. *Member, United Nations.*

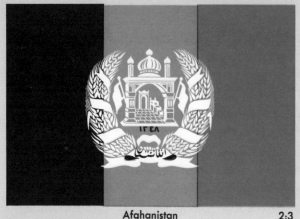

Afghanistan 2:3

Albania 5:7

Algeria 2:3

Andorra 2:3

ALGERIA (al-JEER-ee-yuh): Eleven million people, most of them Moslems, live in this North African country which became an independent republic on July 3, 1962. Before that, it had had various rulers. Arabs conquered it in the seventh century. Beginning in 1518, it was ruled by Turkey, and after 1830, by France. The French language is still permitted, but Arabic is official, replacing French in the schools.

After independence, the National Assembly chose a flag that had been used earlier by revolutionaries. Notice that its crescent differs from those on the flags of some other Moslem countries. Algerians say that the longer horns of their crescent bring better luck than short horns. White in the flag stands for purity, and Algerians believe that green was the favorite color of Mohammed, who always wore a green coat. (See page 137 for more about the crescent.) The official name of the country is Democratic and Popular Republic of Algeria. *Member, United Nations.*

ANDORRA (an-DOR-uh): In A.D. 784, according to tradition, King Charlemagne guaranteed that the people of Andorra could live in freedom; today the country's national anthem still begins with the words, "Great Charlemagne, my father." In 1278, the Catalan Bishop of Urgel and a French count became joint rulers of the country; today the Bishop of Urgel and the President of France are co-princes. France takes care of Andorra's relations with foreign countries.

Possibly because Andorra has two princes, it has two coats of arms. The one that appears on its flag is a shield with a bishop's miter and crosier in one quarter and two cows in another.

Fewer than 15,000 people live in this tiny republic, eighteen miles long and twelve miles wide, wedged between France and Spain in the Pyrenees Mountains and officially named The Valleys of Andorra. Only the heads of families can vote to elect its governing body, the General Council. Council members are not paid, and the country has almost no taxes. But each year the Bishop of Urgel gets 460 Spanish *pesetas* (about $7.75), and France gets 960 *francs* (about $194). Although Andorra has no army, it does have sixteen policemen. If they make an arrest, they must send the prisoner to France, because there is no jail in their country.

Andorrans speak the Catalan language, and they are Roman Catholics. Two radio stations broadcast daily, but there are no newspapers or magazines.

Flags on Ships

On certain special occasions a ship displays all of her flags, including signal flags. Sailors then say she is *dressed*. A ship *wears* flags—she doesn't fly them.

A ship in port may wear flags of two different countries. On a mast, as a courtesy, will be the flag of the country the ship is visiting. The flag of her own country will be displayed at her stern. When a merchant ship leaves port, she will often wear on a mast the flag of the next country she is going to visit. A merchant ship may also wear a *house flag,* the private flag of the company that owns her.

A special kind of naval flag is the *jack*. It is worn on the jackstaff, a flagpole on the bow of a ship. As a rule, only naval vessels wear jacks, and only when they are leaving or entering a port or when tied up to a pier. However, the rules vary from country to country. The United States Union Jack, which consists of fifty white stars in a blue field (the canton of the national flag), is worn on both warships and merchant vessels. Britain's jack is simply the national flag, and many people refer to the British Union Flag as the Union Jack, but that term is technically correct only when the flag is on the jackstaff of a naval vessel.

Argentine cowboys, called gauchos.

ARGENTINA (ar-jen-TEEN-uh): At one time, Argentina was ruled by Spain. When Spain and England were at war, in 1806 and 1807, the British invaded Argentina and tried to capture the city of Buenos Aires. Volunteers in the city formed groups to fight off the British, and one special group chose light blue and white as its colors. Soon blue and white became a symbol of Argentine patriotism.

On the rainy day of May 25, 1810, Argentine patriots again gathered, but this time they were demanding freedom from Spain. As they stood about in one city square, someone handed out blue and white ribbons. Presently word came to the crowd that the viceroy, the Spanish king's representative in Argentina, had resigned. And at that moment, according to legend, the sun burst through the clouds and shone down on the people and their ribbons. In honor of the patriots, the first military flag of independent Argentina had blue and white stripes. It was adopted in 1812. Six years later, the first Congress made it the national flag and added a sun to the middle stripe, recalling the legend about that stormy day in May, 1810. This symbol, called the "Sun of May," still appears in the state flag shown here, but not in the national flag.

About 22,000,000 Argentinians have kept both the language and the Roman Catholic religion of Spain. A few thousand Indians still live around the edges of the country. Those in the northwest speak Quechua, the language of their ancestors whose rich silver mines lured the first

Spanish invaders into the Andes Mountains. (The name Argentina comes from the Latin word for silver.) Officially, the country is called the Argentine Republic. *Member, United Nations.*

AUSTRALIA (aws-TRAIL-yuh): After 1851, a great gold rush began in the southernmost part of the British-ruled continent of Australia. By 1854, the gold miners, who loved independence, were demanding changes in a number of government regulations. They wanted the right to vote. They were angry because a man could not be elected to parliament unless he owned property, and they objected to paying fees for licenses they were supposed to have before they could dig for gold. Many of the protesting miners burned their licenses publicly, then gathered at a fort they called the Eureka Stockade. There they hoisted a flag bearing the stars of a constellation called the Southern Cross, which guides voyagers south of the Equator, just as the North Star guides voyagers in the north. Government troops attacked the Eureka Stockade and killed thirty of the rebels. Immediately the Southern Cross on the miners' flag became an important symbol to Australian workingmen, and it was later used by people who wanted the various colonies in Australia to unite.

In 1901, after the states and territories had agreed to form a kind of union, a national flag-design contest was held. The judges chose, from among 30,000 entries submitted, a design that had been prepared in identical form by three different contestants. One of the three was a schoolboy named Ivor Evans who later became director of a big flag manufacturing company.

In the winning design, which recalled the flag of the Eureka Stockade, the field was blue and included the Southern Cross, as well as a big six-pointed star representing the six states of Australia. The British Union Flag, placed in the canton, showed that the country remained part of the British Empire. A seventh point, representing the territories, was later added to the large star, and in this form the flag remains in use today.

The Commonwealth of Australia has more than 11,000,000 English-speaking citizens. Over one-third of them belong to the Church of England; about one-fourth are Roman Catholic. The rest are divided among a number of other religious groups.

When the first British settlers arrived, Australia had about 300,000 inhabitants who belonged to 500 different tribes, each with its own language. Only about 45,000 descendants of those aboriginal people still remain, together with about 78,000 who have both British and aboriginal ancestors. Most of them live by hunting and fishing on reservations. Technically they have the rights of citizens, but often they are discriminated against. *Member, United Nations.*

Argentina 1:2

Australia 1:2

Austria 2:3

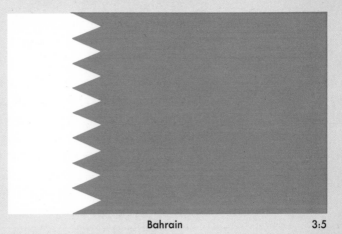

Bahrain 3:5

AUSTRIA (AWS-tree-uh): In 1230, Frederick the Valiant, Duke of Austria, chose a flag that had two red stripes separated by a white stripe. It remained in use, in one way or another, for centuries, and it became the national flag when Austrians established a republic in 1919. At that time they also approved, as a coat of arms, another symbol that had long been in use — an eagle, originally the emblem of a certain nobleman's family in the twelfth century. However, the new republican government changed the eagle in three ways to suggest the hope that three groups in Austria — the middle class, the workers, and the farmers — would remain united. On the eagle's head was a new kind of crown that stood for the middle class, not for royalty. One claw now held a hammer, representing workers. In the other claw was a sickle, which stood for peasants. Austrians like to say that they had the hammer and sickle before these symbols appeared on the flag of any communist country.

The red and white striped flag remained in use until 1938, when the flag of Nazi Germany took its place after Adolf Hitler annexed the country. At the end of World War II the Federal Republic of Austria became independent again and readopted the 1919 national flag. On

23

Sleigh racers, Austria.

the white stripe of the state flag was the eagle wearing a crown and holding the hammer and the sickle, but in addition, a broken chain was shown attached to the eagle's legs, representing the freedom that the 7,250,000 German-speaking Roman Catholic Austrians had won from the Nazis. *Member, United Nations.*

BAHRAIN (bah-RAIN): A chief called a sheik governs a group of islands off the eastern coast of Arabia, the largest of which, Bahrain, gives the country its name.

For centuries the Persians, Turks, Iraqis, Portuguese and others fought over this barren, almost waterless sheikdom. Its pearl fisheries were valuable, and it had a strategic location just opposite the port where an Arab caravan route began. Moreover, the islands could shelter pirates who looted traders in the Persian Gulf. But trade routes changed finally, and pearl fishing declined when Japanese cultured pearls flooded the market. So the islands lost importance until, in 1932, the discovery

Bahraini fisherman casts his traditional net near a modern oil refinery.

of oil made Bahrain one of the richest states in the Middle East. It is so wealthy that everyone who lives there can have free medical care and free education. No one pays taxes of any kind.

The Bahraini flag dates back to the early nineteenth century when a red flag on a ship identified it as an Arab vessel, and gave it some protection at least from Arab pirates. Between 1820 and 1892, the sheiks of Bahrain signed a series of agreements and treaties with Great Britain in which the British pledged to protect Bahrain from foreign enemies. The Bahraini, in return, agreed to give up war and piracy and to stop dealing in slaves. After 1892, the sheiks allowed Britain to conduct their country's foreign affairs. In order to distinguish Bahrain's flag from those of other Arabian states, a vertical white stripe was added to the hoist. (See TRUCIAL STATES.) Sometimes the stripe has a straight edge; sometimes it has eight points, which form a kind of sawtooth edge.

About 185,000 people, most of them Moslems, live on the Bahrain Islands. Five-sixths are native Bahrainis; the others include Pakistanis, Indians, Iranians, Omanis and several hundred British and American oil technicians. Arabic, the official language, is taught in the schools.

BARBADOS (bar-BAY-dohs): This country, the smallest in the Western Hemisphere, became independent from Britain on November 30, 1966, nearly two hundred years after the North American colonies won their revolution. Nevertheless, Barbadians like to say that their tiny island was ahead of the United States in one respect: as early as 1651, it had an agreement with the British guaranteeing that there would be no taxation without representation.

In times of war, Barbados used to give shelter to the British fleet, at other times, to pirates whose old castles can be visited today. Barbadian harbor police still wear the uniform of sailing-ship days, and the emblem on the flag also reflects a seafaring tradition. Its three-pronged fork is the tip of a trident, symbol of the Roman sea god Neptune and formerly a part of the official emblem of Barbados.

The flag's creator had even more than this in mind when he made his design. The island itself, he recalled, had been built up out of the sea by corals growing around a volcano. As for the trident, he decided to use only the tip, broken off from the shaft, to symbolize the island's break with Britain.

Barbados is one of the most densely populated areas in the world. Seventy-nine per cent of the small island's 250,000 people are of African origin. Four per cent are European. Seventeen per cent are mixed. All speak English, and all but about one per cent know how to read and write. Schools can be found in almost every part of the island, although there are only two large towns, one of which is Bridgetown, the capital. Most Barbadians — or "Bajans," as they sometimes call themselves—belong to the Church of England. *Member, United Nations.*

BELGIUM (BELL-jum): This modern country includes three very old and distinct regions—Flanders, Wallonia and Brabant. Ever since the Middle Ages, red has been the important color in the banner of Wallonia; black and yellow were the colors of Flanders; black, yellow and red the colors of Brabant. In 1789, when neighboring France began its great revolution, some of the Belgians also rebelled against their ruler who at that time was the Emperor of Austria. This revolt failed, but before it did, its supporters adopted a flag that contained the colors of all three regions—black, gold and red. Not long afterward, the French general Napoleon conquered Austria and became ruler of the land that is now Belgium. After Napoleon lost power in 1815, the Belgian provinces were ruled by Holland until, in 1830, an explosive revolution was in the making.

Music, so the story goes, touched off the rebellion. One night at the opera the audience was so stirred by a song calling for freedom that men rushed out into the street and started to fight against the Dutch. This time the rebels won, and they adopted the flag that had been used in the first revolt in 1789. The stripes in the flag were horizontal, but they were soon changed to run vertically, and they still do today.

A good many of Belgium's 9,500,000 people are not churchgoers. There is no state religion, but the government helps to pay the salaries of Protestant Evangelical, Catholic, Jewish and Church of England clergymen. Two languages are official—French and Flemish, which is similar to Dutch. Ever since the country became independent, it has been a constitutional monarchy known as the Kingdom of Belgium. *Member, United Nations.*

Woman weaver, Bhutan.

BHUTAN (boo-TAHN): This semi-independent monarchy lies between India and China, high in the Himalaya Mountains. Its ruler is called the Thunder King, or the Dragon King, by his 750,000 subjects, and a wingless dragon—either white or green—appears on the country's flag. The dragon and the red and gold colors come from China. The Indian government has charge of Bhutan's relations with other countries.

Only a few westerners had ever visited Bhutan before 1949. That year, for the first time, an American made the long horseback trip over a steep, narrow trail and discovered that Bhutanese always ride their small ponies uphill, but going downhill they always get off and walk. Since 1949, there has been an automobile road from India.

In Bhutan, as in other parts of the Himalayas, people keep herds of yaks. They make cheese from the milk, use yak butter as flavoring for their tea, and ship yak tails to other countries to be made into beards for Santa Claus costumes. Long ago, the tails had another use—as decorations on the poles of flags that some Asian warriors carried in battle.

The Bhutanese are Mongols, and their language is a dialect of Tibetan. Their religion is a variety of Buddhism.

26

Barbados   2:3

Belgium   13:15

Bhutan   1:1

Bolivia   2:3

BOLIVIA (bo-LIV-ee-yuh): This is a land of contrasts, contradictions and surprises. Steamships sail along one border, yet nowhere does Bolivia touch the sea. The reason—its shore is the edge of Lake Titicaca, one of the largest lakes in the world and 12,500 feet above sea level. Instead of one capital, Bolivia has two—the city of Sucre, the "legal capital," and La Paz, the "seat of the government," where the president lives and where the congress meets. The country is named for its revolutionary hero Simón Bolívar—although he was a Venezuelan, not a Bolivian. In the mountains near the city of Potosí, Indian silver mines once produced immense treasure that the Spaniards carried away. Eventually Spanish rule ended, and the silver gave out—but something even more useful, tin ore, now comes from the mines.

The state flag reflects both the land of Bolivia and its history. Its colors stand for the riches to be found there: red for its animals, yellow for the minerals, green for its many different plants and trees. The coat of arms shows these same things and more. A breadfruit tree and a sheaf of grain symbolize lowland and highland crops. From the alpaca's fleece come expensive yarns. The mountain represents mining. And there are laurel leaves for victory, an olive branch for peace, a red cap

27

Bolivian Indian women in the market place.

for liberty (see page 38), a battle-ax for the Inca Indians who ruled much of Bolivia long ago, nine stars for the nine departments or regions, and the huge bird called the condor which lives in the Andes Mountains. This coat of arms does not appear on the national flag.

There is freedom of religion in Bolivia, although the Roman Catholic church has official recognition. Spanish is the official language, but more than half of the 3,550,000 people speak Indian languages, instead. *Member, United Nations.*

BOTSWANA (bah-TSWAH-nuh): The original inhabitants of Botswana were Bushmen, a people who have brownish skins. About 24,000 of their descendants still live in the huge Kalahari Desert, very much as all human beings lived in the Stone Age. Today most of the 560,000 people in Botswana are descended from black-skinned Negroes who have invaded the homeland of the Bushmen from time to time during the last 1500 years. The Negroes belong to eight tribes, each of which has its own language. English was made the official government language when the Republic of Botswana became independent in 1966. (Before that, for almost eighty years, Botswana had been known as the Bechuanaland Protectorate and was under British rule.) One person out of seven is Christian. The rest practice traditional tribal religions.

28

When Botswana's Legislative Assembly chose a flag, it took care to avoid color combinations that were already used by any of the eight tribes. The result was a flag of blue, white and black. Blue represents the sky and the hope for water. Black stands for the Negro people, who are the majority, white for the European minority (about 3,000 people, most of whom are farmers). The flag as a whole stands for tribal and racial equality and national unity. *Member, United Nations.*

BRAZIL (bruh-ZIL) became an independent country when it separated from the Portuguese Empire in 1822. This new country also called itself an empire, and it placed a crown as part of the coat of arms in the center of its flag.

A revolution overthrew the empire in 1889. The new republican government removed the crown from the flag and put stars and a sphere in its place, together with a motto that means "Order and Progress." The five large stars represent the Southern Cross, the same constellation that appears on the Australian flag but shown as it looks to people in the city of Rio de Janeiro. These five stars, plus eighteen smaller ones, stand for the Brazilian territories and the twenty-three states. The green and yellow colors in the flag symbolize farming and mining. Blue represents the first Portuguese pioneers; the white band, the path of the moon and the planets across the sky.

Brazil is the fifth largest country in the world. More than half of its 82,000,000 people have pure European ancestry; about one-tenth are pure African. About one-quarter are mixed European and African, and some of these are also part American Indian. The only remaining pure Indians live in small scattered groups in isolated places, and their number keeps dwindling.

In the year 1500, when the Portuguese added Brazil to their empire, the only people who lived there were Indians. They spoke so many different languages that Jesuit missionaries made up a new language which they and all Indians could use. Most Brazilians now speak Portuguese. Although church and government are separate, the United States of Brazil is considered a Roman Catholic country. A number of old African religions also have followers, and a great many people practice a faith that combines African and Catholic beliefs. *Member, United Nations.*

BRUNEI (broo-NIGH) shares the large island of Borneo with Indonesia and the Malaysian states of Sarawak (pronounced suh-RAH-wuk) and Sabah.* The majority of its 100,000 people are Malays; about one-fourth are of Chinese descent, and less than one-fifth belong to various small tribes. The official religion is Islam, the Moslem faith, to which most of the non-Chinese belong. Many of the tribesmen practice their traditional

The old and the new in Brazil.

*In 1968 the Philippines laid claim to Sabah.

religions. The official language is Malay, although Indonesian, Dutch, English and tribal languages are also spoken.

The yellow of Brunei's flag stands for the sultan, or prince, who rules this land of ancient river boats and modern oil wells. The broad white band in the flag is the color of the First Minister of State, and the narrow black band represents the Second Minister of State.

Four hundred years ago the sultanate of Brunei was very much larger than it is today. Then the Spaniards conquered it, and after they left, its rulers never regained much power. Since 1888 the country has been a protectorate of Great Britain. This means that the British manage its foreign affairs. Brunei received a constitution in 1959, but a British advisor (called a High Commissioner) still has great influence in the government's activities.

BULGARIA (buhl-GARE-ee-yuh): Late in the fourteenth century the empire of Turkey conquered neighboring Bulgaria. After that, for nearly five hundred years, Turks ruled the country. In 1878, Bulgaria became partially independent and adopted a flag of its own for the first time. The white stripe stood for freedom, the green for agriculture and the red for bravery.

During the two World Wars, Bulgarian kings allied themselves with Germany, but in 1944, before World War II ended, there was a revolution, led by five political parties, including the Communist. Bulgaria then began to fight against Germany. In 1946 the country voted to abolish the monarchy, and a communist became Prime Minister. At the same time, a constitution was adopted — something Bulgaria had never had before.

The constitution gave the country a new name, the People's Republic of Bulgaria, and a new flag based on the old one. The colors in the flag remained the same, but in the top (white) stripe next to the hoist there was added a coat of arms — a golden lion surrounded by sheaves of grain. Above this device is a red star, and below it the date, September 9, 1944, the day of the communist revolution.

The 8,000,000 people in this socialist country speak the Bulgarian language. Most of those who practice a religion belong to the Eastern Orthodox Church; there are also some Roman Catholics, Protestants and Moslems. The government itself is non-religious. *Member, United Nations.*

Some Bulgarians still wear traditional costumes at festivals.

30

Botswana   2:3

Brazil   7:10

Brunei   1:2

Bulgaria   2:3

Burma   5:9

BURMA (BURR-muh): In the eleventh century A.D., Buddhist kings ruled this country in southeast Asia. Today, Buddhism is still the official religion, but the Union of Burma is a republic with certain socialist features. (Important industries, for example, are owned by the government.) Three-fourths of the 25,000,000 inhabitants speak some dialect of Burmese, the official language. English is also widely used by the government. One-fourth of the people belong to many separate groups speaking more than a hundred different languages.

Beginning in 1619, the British opened trading posts in Burma, and by 1886 they ruled the whole country, as well as neighboring India. In 1937, they started work on a road which was to cross the mountains

31

Inner courtyard, main pagoda, Rangoon, Burma.

into China. These mountains are so steep that the road had to wind for 717 miles in order to go 204 miles as the crow flies. Later, during World War II, supplies were sent over the Burma Road to help Chinese armies fight against invading Japanese armies.

In 1942, Japan conquered Burma and the road was closed, but many Burmans kept on fighting as guerillas, and they designed their own flag, which had a big white star. Burma became fully independent in January, 1948, and the white star of the guerilla flag was made part of the national flag. White stands for purity, truth and steadfastness. The smaller stars around the big one represent various minority groups. Blue is for the sky at night, red for courage, determination and unity.

A Burmese Buddhist, U Thant, became Acting Secretary-General of the United Nations in 1961. He later was made Secretary-General and was elected to a second five-year term of office when his first term ended. *Member, United Nations.*

BURUNDI (boor-UN-dee), which lies on the slopes of the Mountains of the Moon in Africa, gained its independence from Belgium on July 1, 1962. In that same year, Burundi adopted a flag. The red in it stands for the sacrifices of those who fought for freedom. The green is for progress and hope, and the white for peace for all mankind. In the center of the flag are three stars with green borders. Originally the

32

emblems in the center were a drum, ancient symbol of royalty, and a stalk of sorghum. When the king was overthrown in 1966, the drum was removed. Later the stars replaced the sorghum stalk.

Most of the 3,000,000 Burundians come from one of three tribes —the very tall Batusi (or Watusi or Tutsi), the very short Batwa (or Twa), and the medium-sized Bahutu (or Hutu). Many members of all these tribes also live in the neighboring country of Rwanda. About 85 per cent of the Burundians are Hutu, but for a long time they were ruled by the Batusi minority. The Hutu were actually serfs who had to care for the cattle that belonged to the Batusi. The Hutu have now rebelled against this serfdom and killed a great many of their Batusi rulers. Both the Hutu and the Batusi speak Kirundi, which is often called Burundian and is an official language. French is also official, and many people speak Swahili, too. About half the Burundians worship a god called Imana, which means "The Principle of Good." The other half are Christians, mostly Roman Catholic. *Member, United Nations.*

CAMBODIA (cam-BO-dee-uh): In the year 623, according to the Buddhist calendar (A.D. 80, according to the Western calendar), the king of Cambodia chose a flag similar to the one still in use today. Blue in the flag stands for the ruler's power and authority. White represents faith in him. Red stands for the willingness of Cambodians to die for king and country. The design in the center shows the ancient temple, Angkor Wat, which has a curious history.

There was once a city called Angkor, built between A.D. 800 and 1300 by kings who considered themselves gods. The city stretched out for five miles in one direction, six in the other, and in and around it stood temples covered with the most intricate, lively carvings. Angkor Wat was one of the grandest of them. At first, people worshiped Brahma in the temples. Later, Angkor Wat became sacred to Buddha. (Buddhism is still the country's official religion.) Not long after 1300, a change began to affect the country. Perhaps the irrigation systems failed or the land became less fertile. Or there may have been a destructive flood. At any rate, Cambodia lost much of its vigor. It was defeated by armies from Siam, and Angkor was abandoned after 1432. From then on, says the national anthem, "the temples slept in the forest." Jungle growth covered the ruined city, and only a few people remembered Angkor Wat. Four hundred years later, in 1858, an amazed French explorer came upon the ruins, which archeologists have now cleared and partially restored.

A village wedding party in Cambodia.

Cambodia came under French rule in 1863, but the king was allowed to keep his throne. In 1947, the king ceased to be an absolute monarch and began to rule under a constitution. Six years later, Cambodia declared its independence from France. In 1960, Prince Sihanouk

33

became head of state but refused to be crowned king. His country's 5,700,000 inhabitants speak Cambodian, also called Khmer. Many of the people also know French and English. *Member, United Nations.*

CAMEROON (kam-err-OON): This part of the western coast of Africa was the home of two hundred independent tribes until Germany began to rule the country in 1884. During World War I, in 1916, France took the eastern part of this colony from Germany, and Britain took the western part. French Cameroon became independent on January 1, 1960, and the south portion of British Cameroon won independence on October 1, 1961. These regions then united to form the Federal Republic of Cameroon and adopted their present flag.

To the people of Cameroon, the green in the flag stands for hope and for tropical plants that grow in the southern part of the country. Red is the color of authority and stands for the unity and independence of the nation's separate regions. Yellow is for the soil of the North and also for wealth and for the sun, which Cameroonians say is the "source of the people's glory." (Farming is their most important activity.) The two stars symbolize the two federated states.

About one-tenth of the 6,000,000 Cameroonians are Christians and one-tenth Moslems; the rest practice some form of traditional tribal religion. Many quite different African languages are spoken. In East Cameroon, French is the official language for schools and the government; in West Cameroon, English is official. *Member, United Nations.*

Harvesting cocoa in Cameroon.

More About Flags on Ships

An *ensign* is a special flag usually worn at the stern of a warship. In the Middle Ages, when a nobleman was in command of a ship of war, he hung his personal flag from the stern for identification. It was called his *insignia,* but gradually the word changed to *ensign,* and the meaning of the flag itself changed, too. It no longer identifies a person, but shows the country from which the naval vessel comes. Great Britain, Norway, the Soviet Union and a number of other countries have specially designed ensigns that are distinct from their national flags.

Striking—that is, hauling down the ensign during battle—is a sign of surrender. With that in mind, the commander of a British warship has often gone into battle with two or three ensigns showing, so that if one is shot away, nobody will jump to the wrong conclusion.

The United States, France and some other countries have no special ensigns. They use their national flags on naval vessels.

34

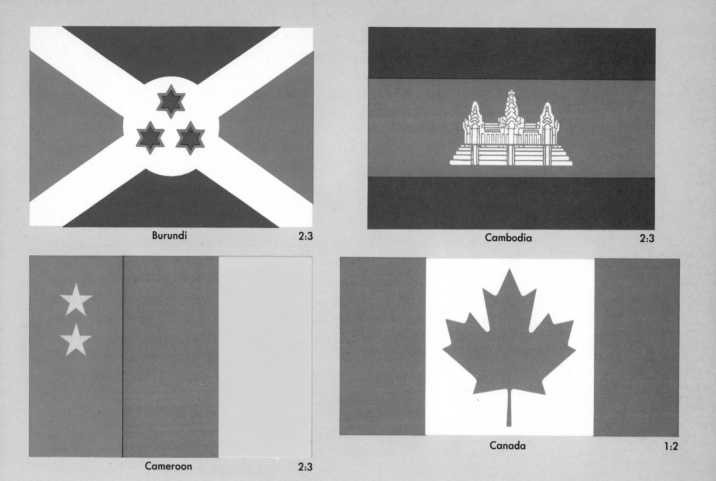

Burundi   2:3

Cambodia   2:3

Cameroon   2:3

Canada   1:2

CANADA (CAN-uh-duh): More than fifty years ago, some Canadians began to say that they wanted a new flag — one that showed no connections with any other country. (At that time, Canada was part of the British Empire, and the Canadian flag had the British Union Flag in the canton.) After World War II, there was more and more talk about the flag. The government considered over four thousand different designs, and finally, in 1964, after the longest debate in the history of the Canadian parliament, a new one was adopted. The design in the center of the flag is a maple leaf, which is the national emblem. By now, the British Empire had become the Commonwealth of Nations, with Queen Elizabeth II at its head. Since Canada was a member of the Commonwealth, the country waited for the Queen to make the flag official by a Royal Proclamation in 1965.

Among the nearly 20,000,000 Canadians, about 6,000,000 speak French as their first language, and both French and English are official languages. Some public schools are Catholic and the teaching is done in French. Others are Protestant, and are conducted in English. In addition, Canada has many inhabitants descended from German, Ukrainian, Scandinavian, Dutch, Polish, Jewish, Hungarian and Italian immigrants. Eskimos in the Far North and scattered groups of Indians together number 220,000.

Only one country in the world, the U.S.S.R., covers a larger area than Canada. The Canadian border, alongside the United States, stretches for nearly four thousand miles across the North American continent. There have been no fortifications on either side of this border for more than a hundred years. *Member, United Nations.*

CENTRAL AFRICAN REPUBLIC: About 1,400,000 people live on the high plateau-land of this country which lies just north of the Equator. Aside from 6,000 Europeans, all the Central Africans belong to one of four tribal groups, each with its own language and religious beliefs. When members of different tribes want to talk to each other, they use a special intertribal tongue called Sangho. No one is sure just when the four tribes moved into the area. They seem to have been there when French soldiers and explorers arrived in 1889. By 1894, France had made the country a colony and called it Ubangi-Shari. On August 13, 1960, it became the independent Central African Republic. French continued to be the official language.

In 1958, as the country was preparing for independence, lawmakers approved a flag design unlike any other in existence — a vertical stripe of one color crossing four horizontal stripes of different colors. *Member, United Nations.*

Students in the Technical College, Central African Republic.

CEYLON (see-LAHN): In prehistoric times a group of Stone Age people moved onto this large island near the coast of India, and a few of their descendants still live there. Many other immigrants have arrived since then. The largest group, the Sinhalese, are believed to have come from northern India in the sixth century B.C. They kept their own language, and for a long time they had kings who flew a dark red flag with a yellow lion on it.

A farmer and his children go to market in Ceylon.

Tamil people came from southern India with a different language, possibly in the fourteenth century A.D. Arabs, Malays, Portuguese and Dutch also invaded the island. In 1796, the British overthrew the Dutch and ruled until 1948, when Ceylon became independent.

The 11,000,000 Ceylonese include more than 7,000,000 Sinhalese who are Buddhists, about 1,200,000 Tamils who are Hindus, nearly 700,000 Christians and 1,650,000 Moslems.

The Ceylonese flag adopted in 1950 is based on the old lion flag of the Sinhalese kings, to which were added a saffron stripe representing the Tamil-speaking group and a green stripe for the Moslems. Sinhalese is the official language, but in 1966 the Tamils won the right to do business in their own language. Education from kindergarten through university is free. *Member, United Nations.*

37

CHAD (rhymes with LAD) takes its name from Lake Chad, a very large, very shallow body of water that has no outlet. Northeast of the lake, the Sahara Desert has been slowly spreading over the land. Here, in a few places, lie water holes where nomads bring sheep, donkeys and large herds of camels to drink. The source of the water is unknown, for very little rain falls in the desert. Even when the camels drink a hole almost dry during the day, it fills up again during the night. Equally strange are the crocodiles that often appear in the holes. They must live in caves beneath the desert.

Chad has visible caves where prehistoric men made carvings and paintings on the stone walls. These pictures show giraffes, elephants, big cats, and hunters with bows and arrows, which can only mean that long ago this was a land of grass and trees. Great forests and grassy plains still cover the southern part of the country. The Chadians who live on the desert in the north are Moslems. Elsewhere they follow various older tribal religions.

France seized Chad when it was building an empire in Africa, and the country remained under French rule until 1960, when it became the independent Republic of Chad. The official language is still French, but most of the 4,000,000 people speak one of several tribal languages.

In 1959, while Chad was preparing for independence, it adopted a three-colored flag. The blue in it stands for the sky and hope and life. Yellow is the color of the sun which lights the land. Red is the color of fire and symbolizes the unity of the different kinds of people in the country. *Member, United Nations.*

The Liberty Cap

In ancient Rome, tens of thousands of people were slaves. Sometimes a few of them were given their freedom, especially in the first and second centuries A.D. As a sign that they had become their own masters, they took to wearing a special kind of cap with a long top that drooped to one side.

Some Frenchmen remembered these ancient liberty caps in 1791, in the midst of their revolution, and people began to wear them again as a sign that they wanted to be free from the rule of the king. The French caps were usually red, the color of the flag that Frenchmen had raised as a symbol of revolution.

When people in Latin America won independence from the King of Spain, some of them recalled the red Liberty Cap of the French Revolution. That is why this symbol is part of the coats of arms of several countries in Central and South America.

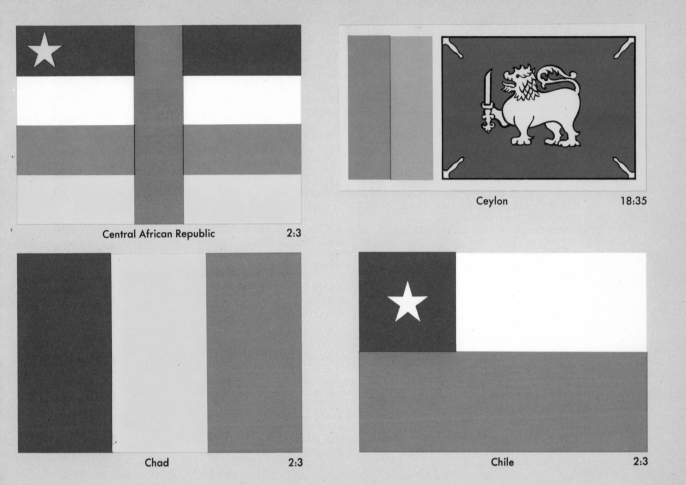

Central African Republic 2:3

Ceylon 18:35

Chad 2:3

Chile 2:3

CHILE (CHILL-ee) has the highest mountain and the driest desert in the Western Hemisphere, besides rich farming land and more industry than most other South American nations. It stretches out in a longer thinner shape than any other country, reaching from the tropics to icy Antarctic seas. And it owns the Juan Fernández Islands in the Pacific Ocean where a castaway sailor had adventures that led to the writing of the story of *Robinson Crusoe*.

In November, 1818, Chile became independent of Spain and adopted the flag it still flies. Red in the flag stands for the blood shed by those who fought for independence. White is for the snow in the high Andes Mountains. Blue is for the sky overhead. The star guides the country toward honor and progress, and it also stands for the country's Indian minority.

There are less than 150,000 pure Indians left in Chile. They belong to three groups: the Changos fish along the northern coast; the Araucanians live in the Andes Mountains, and the Fuegians wander in the cold lands of the far south. Among the 8,600,000 other inhabitants, most members of the upper class are descended from the Roman Catholic

39

Chilean boys help a fisherman unload boat.

Spaniards and Basques who conquered the country in the sixteenth century. Some have Irish and German ancestry, mixed with Spanish. Some in the working class are part Spanish and part Indian. Spanish is the official language. *Member, United Nations.*

CHINA: Long before Europe had any printed books, the Chinese invented a way to set type and print from it. They were the first to make many other inventions, such as the compass and a rig for drilling oil wells. But then Chinese creativity lagged. The later emperors who ruled the country kept out the new ideas of science and industry and democracy that developed in many parts of the world.

In the nineteenth century, Britain and other western countries began to control areas in China; many Chinese who wanted their country to be independent and up-to-date had to flee. Some went to Hawaii. There, in 1894, a Chinese refugee named Sun Yat-sen started a revolutionary organization. By 1908, his group had grown and adopted a flag which its members used in 1911 when they rebelled against the government of the Chinese Empire. The next year they established, in part of China, the first republic in Asia.

40

The colors of the flag stood for what are called the Three Principles of the People. Blue means equality, justice and democracy. White means fraternity, frankness and a livelihood for the people. Red stands for liberty, sacrifice and nationalism. The twelve points of the white sun represent the twelve hours of a clock, and the sun itself is a symbol of progress.

By 1926, the revolution had spread throughout the whole country, and the government of the Republic of China officially adopted the flag of Sun Yat-sen's group. Later, a new revolution began when many people grew dissatisfied with the government of the republic. Taking their flag with them, officials of the republic fled in 1949 from the mainland of China to the island which the Chinese call Taiwan.

Taiwan now has about 13,000,000 inhabitants. Of these, 150,000 are related to the Malaysians. They belong to a number of tribes, each with its own language. If members of different tribes want to talk to each other, they speak Japanese, which they learned while the Japanese ruled Taiwan from 1895 until the end of World War II. Ten million of the people on Taiwan are Chinese who came from South China long ago, bringing their own dialect with them. In 1949, about 2,000,000 supporters of the Republic of China moved onto Taiwan. Their leaders spoke Mandarin Chinese, which was originally the language of North

Chinese celebrating
National Day in Peking.

China. Now the schools on Taiwan use Mandarin Chinese, which is also the official language.

Taiwan's aboriginal inhabitants still practice their tribal religions. The majority of the Chinese on the island are either Buddhist or Taoist, and there are also Christians. The Republic of China, which now governs only Taiwan, is a member of the United Nations, and holds China's seat as a permanent member of the Security Council of the United Nations.

The People's Republic of China is the name used by the Communist government on the mainland. In the red flag which it adopted a large gold star represented its program. The four small stars stood for peasants, workers, small businessmen and Chinese capitalists whose help the country needed. The red stood for revolution, but, like the gold in the star, it is also a traditional Chinese color.

About 760,000,000 people — one-fourth of all the inhabitants of the world — live in mainland China. Ninety per cent of them are called Han Chinese, and Mandarin Chinese is their official language. The other 10 per cent are divided among about fifty other nationalities, many of which have their own languages.

Before the communist revolution in 1949, most of the Chinese had beliefs that were a mixture of Buddhist, Taoist and Confucian teachings. A few million were pure Buddhists. There were about 50,000,000 Moslems and about 4,000,000 Christians. Because the new government began to discourage all religion when it came to power, it is hard to know exactly how strong these various beliefs are today.

Lessons broadcast by radio are taught to this Colombian class for young and old.

COLOMBIA (ko-LUM-bee-yuh): Spaniards built their first permanent settlement in Colombia in 1525, and representatives of Spain's king ruled over the area for nearly three hundred years. In 1810, the Colombians began a war for independence. As they fought, they carried a yellow, blue and red flag that had been designed in 1806 by the revolutionary hero Francisco Miranda. (See ECUADOR and VENEZUELA.) The rebels won their war in 1819 and established a republic which at first was called New Granada. At the same time, they adopted a slight variation of the flag they had carried in battle. This is still the flag that flies over the Republic of Colombia. Its yellow stripe stands for wealth, independence and justice; the blue is for loyalty; the red is for courage, honor and the blood shed by patriots.

Most of the 15,000,000 Colombians are Roman Catholics, either Spanish in origin or part Spanish and part Indian. Some are also part Negro, and there are 110,000 pure Indians who speak their own language. Spanish is used officially. *Member, United Nations.*

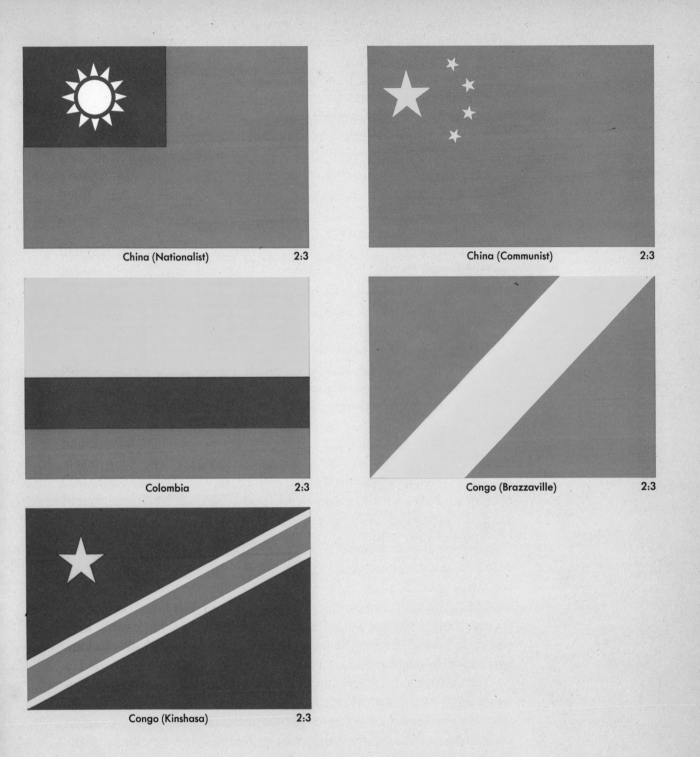

China (Nationalist) 2:3

China (Communist) 2:3

Colombia 2:3

Congo (Brazzaville) 2:3

Congo (Kinshasa) 2:3

CONGO (Brazzaville): The capital of this former French colony is the city of Brazzaville, and so the country itself is usually called Congo (Brazzaville) to distinguish it from its neighbor, Congo (Kinshasa). The full name of Congo (Brazzaville) is the Republic of the Congo.

In 1959, as the country was preparing to be an independent state, its leaders adopted the flag which came into use on August 15, 1960. In 1965, the government began to call itself socialist.

43

The Congolese—nearly a million—belong to several different tribes. A small number are Pygmies. Each tribe has its own language and traditional religion. French is the official language of the government. *Member, United Nations.*

CONGO (Kinshasa): In 1876, Leopold II, King of Belgium, started a company to carry on trading and mining in a part of Africa through which the Congo River flows. For many years the king, acting as a private businessman, claimed ownership of this very large territory. Then, in 1908, the Congo lands became a colony claimed by the Belgian government. In 1960, the 15,000,000 Congolese people won independence from Belgium and established a government they called the Democratic Republic of the Congo. The city of Léopoldville, which became the country's capital, has been renamed Kinshasa.

The blue in the flag stands for hope. Yellow is for prosperity. The star symbolizes the goal of the two hundred tribes, which is unity, and the red stripe stands for the blood shed by Congolese as they sought that goal.

About one-third of the Congolese are Roman Catholics; the rest follow tribal religions. The principal languages are Swahili and Lingala. *Member, United Nations.*

COSTA RICA (cos-ta ree-ka): The present flag is the seventh that Costa Rica has had since it declared independence from Spain. The colors blue and white have been in all of them since August, 1823. A red stripe was added in 1848, together with the coat of arms which was changed slightly in 1906. Blue stands for the sky and the oceans. Red is for the blood that Costa Ricans have shed in fighting for liberty. White stands for peace, which the country takes seriously; its army was abolished by the constitution in 1949.

On the state flag, a rising sun in the coat of arms represents the newness of the country. The three peaks indicate that it is mountainous. Two sailing ships mean that it touches the Pacific Ocean on one side and the Caribbean Sea on the other. Green leaves stand for the fertility of the land and the glory of its past. The five stars are for the five Central American countries that were united for a short time in the nineteenth century. (For that story, see EL SALVADOR.) The national flag does not have the coat of arms.

About 1,400,000 people live in the Republic of Costa Rica. Roman Catholicism is their religion, Spanish is their language, and most of them are of pure Spanish ancestry. There has been little intermarriage with Indians, who number only a few thousand and who keep their own lan-

guages and religions. Several thousand Negroes have come to Costa Rica from the British West Indies.

Costa Ricans—they call themselves "Ticos"—like to say that they have more schools than policemen. All education is free. All citizens of voting age, both men and women, are required by law to vote. *Member, United Nations.*

Costa Rica: (left) a guide near Irazu Volcano; (right) women workers sorting coffee beans.

CUBA was one of the places where Christopher Columbus stopped on his first voyage to the New World, and he noted that the island had great natural wealth and a pleasant climate. It also turned out to be one of the very few tropical regions in the world where there are no poisonous snakes.

Although Cuba quickly became a Spanish possession, it was the last of Spain's American colonies to win freedom. For one reason, it is an island, and the other newly independent Latin American countries did not dare to send aid to it in the face of the powerful Spanish navy. Nevertheless, throughout the nineteenth century, Cubans were often in revolt, partly to achieve independence and partly to end slavery, which was finally abolished in 1886.

The Cuban flag was designed in 1849 by two exiles living in New York City. Its three blue stripes represent the three provinces into which the country was divided in colonial times. The white stripes are for purity and peace, the red triangle for blood shed by Cuban patriots. The three sides of the triangle symbolize Liberty, Equality and Fraternity. The white Lone Star represents the unity of the people and the nation's independence. This flag was first flown in 1859, then again in other unsuccessful revolts and in the final war for liberation, led by the poet José Martí, which ended in 1898 when the United States went to war with Spain and captured the island. The Cubans were granted independence by the United States in 1902.

Cuba's 7,260,000 people speak Spanish and most of them can read

45

Cuban dance students perform.

and write. They are largely Roman Catholic, although a great many do not practice their faith. There are also several hundred thousand Protestants and a smaller number of Jews. Other important religions are a blend of Christianity and beliefs that came from Africa with the slaves. More than one-fifth of the people are Negro or of mixed Negro-European descent, and there is a Cuban saying that goes "We are all *café con leche* (coffee with milk); some have more coffee, some have more milk."

Cuba is the only country in the Western Hemisphere where communists are in power. *Member, United Nations.*

A shepherd in Cyprus.

CYPRUS (SIGH-prus): Few countries on earth have had more foreign rulers than the Republic of Cyprus. Powerful nations have wanted this island because ships from its ports could easily attack any other ships in the eastern end of the Mediterranean Sea. Whoever controlled Cyprus also controlled trade in that part of the world.

People also wanted Cyprus because of its copper mines. In fact, the name Cyprus comes from the Greek word for copper. Ancient Greeks may have been the first outsiders to conquer the island. Then came Phoenicians, Assyrians, Egyptians, Persians, Greeks again, Romans,

46

Costa Rica 2:3

Cuba 1:2

Cyprus 3:5

Czechoslovakia 2:3

Moslems, Crusaders, Venetians, Turks, and in 1878, the British.

On August 16, 1960, after a fierce war, Cyprus won independence from Britain and established a republic, with Archbishop Makarios of the Cyprus Orthodox Church as President. A Turk was named Vice-President. Four-fifths of the population are Greek-speaking Christians. One-fifth are Turkish-speaking Moslems.

Most Cypriots, as both Greeks and Turks are called, also speak English. The flag, adopted in 1960, shows a map of Cyprus, under which are olive branches symbolizing peace. *Member, United Nations.*

CZECHOSLOVAKIA (CHECK-oh-slo-VAK-ee-yuh): When World War I began in 1914, many different groups of people in the central part of Europe were ruled by the Emperor of Austria-Hungary. Each of these groups had its own language and customs. Two of them, the Czechs and the Slovaks, joined together at the end of the war, and in 1918 they formed a republic with a flag of white and red. In 1920, blue was added. These were the colors in ancient flags of the kingdoms of Bohemia and Moravia that had once controlled parts of the new republic's territory.

47

Both the Czechs and the Slovaks had formerly used these colors when they made unsuccessful attempts to win freedom.

Before World War II, the armies of Nazi Germany occupied the country. Three years after they were driven out, Czechoslovakia became the Czechoslovakian People's Republic, with communists holding the most important offices in the government. The country is now called the Czechoslovak Socialist Republic. The flag remains the same as the one adopted in 1918.

There are about 13,000,000 Czechs and Slovaks, plus minority groups totaling about 1,000,000. Both the Czech and Slovak languages are official. About three-fourths of the people are Roman Catholic, the others, Eastern Orthodox, Protestant, or Jewish. *Member, United Nations.*

Czechoslovakian folk dancers.

DAHOMEY (dah-HO-mee): For a long time the land that now makes up Dahomey was divided into several small kingdoms. After European traders reached that part of Africa in the fifteenth century, the kings grew rich selling slaves. In the nineteenth century, a descendant of one of the early rulers dominated the other monarchies and brought them all together in the Kingdom of Dahomey. His success came as a result of the army he organized. It was large and powerful, and many of the soldiers were women who used their weapons with great skill. In 1851, the king signed a trade agreement with the French. In 1883, France began to take control of the country, and by the end of the century it was a French colony. It became the independent Republic of Dahomey and adopted its own flag in 1960.

The red band in the flag stands for the color of the soil. Yellow is for the plains, called savannas, in one part of the country. Green stands

A farmer in Dahomey.

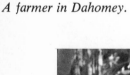

for trees, especially the abundant palm groves that give Dahomey much of its wealth today. Palm oil is sold abroad, mostly for soap making; karite nuts from Dahomey's mountains are used in the making of lipstick.

The 2,300,000 Dahomeans are divided into eight main tribal groups, each of which has its own language and religious beliefs. French is the official language of the government and schools. *Member, United Nations.*

DENMARK (DEN-mark) is a very old European monarchy, and it flies the oldest of Europe's flags. To the Danes, their flag is so special that it has its own name, *Dannebrog,* probably meaning "red cloth." According to legend, the Dannebrog came down from heaven in A.D. 1219 and brought victory to Danish armies that were far from home, invading Estonia, now one of the republics in the Soviet Union. No one really knows just when the flag was first used, but it certainly existed before the end of the fourteenth century. At that time the Danish Queen Margrethe united her country with Norway and Sweden and adopted

Danish schoolgirls learn to cook.

49

a coat of arms that had three crowns. Later, after Sweden withdrew from the Union, Swedish and Danish kings got into an argument because Denmark still used the three-crown emblem. The disagreement was one of the reasons given for a seven-year war between them.

Denmark has a great many colorful emblems that originated in the Middle Ages. It also has a long seafaring history. Both traditions were of such interest to King Frederick IX when he was young that he had anchors, wreaths and dragons tattooed on his chest and arms.

There are more than 1,400 libraries in Denmark, about one for every 3,300 people, as well as a number of library boats that travel to small islands. Careful records are kept, and the government pays an author according to the number of his books on the library shelves.

Most of the 4,750,000 Danes speak Danish. Two groups have their own languages: the 25,000 Eskimos in Greenland, which belongs to Denmark, and the 35,000 people on Denmark's Faroe Islands, north of Scotland, who speak Faroese. The official religion of the country is Evangelical Lutheran, but all religions are permitted. *Member, United Nations.*

DOMINICAN (do-MIN-ee-can) **REPUBLIC:** Two nations — the Dominican Republic and Haiti—now share the island of Hispaniola which Christopher Columbus visited in 1492. For a time, after it was discovered, the whole island was a Spanish colony called Santo Domingo. Then the French seized the western part that came to be called Haiti. In 1822, after the Spanish-speaking Dominicans had won independence from Spain, the Haitians invaded the Dominican area and tried to force everyone to speak French. Finally the Haitians made life so miserable that the Dominicans rebelled. By 1844, they had regained their independence. Spanish is still their language.

During the revolt, the Dominican leader, Juan Pablo Duarte, had a slogan which also served as a secret password: *"Dios, Patria y Libertad,"* meaning, "God, Fatherland and Liberty." Because there were three parts to the slogan, Duarte's group came to be known as *La Trinitaria,* the Trinity. So the present Dominican flag, which he designed, is called the Trinitarian flag. The red in it symbolizes the blood and fire of revolutions; blue is for liberty; and the white cross stands for sacrifices in the cause of freedom. In the coat of arms at the center of the flag, the Bible and cross are symbols of the Roman Catholic Church, to which most of the people belong.

In spite of the Dominicans' history of warfare against dictators and invasions by Haiti, Spain and the United States, the population has grown from 54,000 at the beginning of the nineteenth century to over 3,600,000. More than three-fourths of the people are Negro or of mixed Negro and European ancestry. *Member, United Nations.*

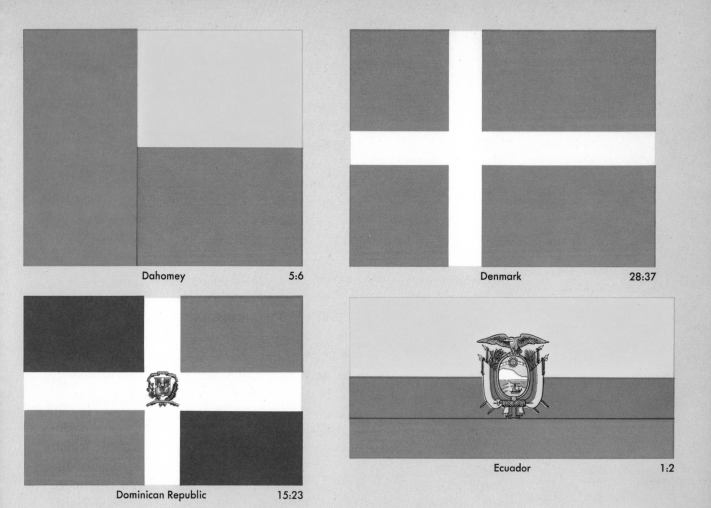

Dahomey   5:6

Denmark   28:37

Dominican Republic   15:23

Ecuador   1:2

ECUADOR (EK-wah-dor): The land that is now Ecuador won independence from Spain and flew the flag of revolutionary heroes Simón Bolívar and Francisco Miranda in 1822. For a while it became part of a larger country called *Gran Colombia* (see COLOMBIA and VENEZUELA), then withdrew and became a separate country. Since that time, Ecuador has had many flags.

In the center of the coat of arms on the present state flag there appears one of the very early steamships which had a paddle wheel and sails, too, in case the new-fangled machinery should break down. Behind it rises the highest peak in the country. Ecuadorians say the yellow in their flag stands for sunshine, grain and wealth. Blue stands for rivers, the ocean and the sky; red is for the blood of patriots who fought to win freedom and justice.

More than 5,000,000 people live in the Republic of Ecuador. One-third are pure Indian. Some belong to the very primitive Jívaro tribe that practices head-hunting as part of its religion. Other Ecuadorian Indians are descended from the Incas. About one-third of the people are part Indian and part Spanish. Only a few are of pure European or

51

pure Negro origin. In one city, Esmeraldas, live descendants of slaves who revolted against their owners in 1533 and then established a small Negro empire. One part of Ecuador—the Galápagos Islands, which lie five hundred miles out in the Pacific Ocean—had no inhabitants except huge turtles, lizards, birds and other animals until recently. A few people live there now.

The language of the Ecuadorian government and the schools is Spanish, but many Indians speak only an Indian language. Except for those Indians who practice ancient religions, most of the people are Roman Catholics. *Member, United Nations.*

(Left) A market place in Ecuador; (right) Rope is made in El Salvador by Indians who still use ancient methods.

EL SALVADOR (el SAL-vuh-dor): Along with Guatemala, Honduras, Nicaragua and Costa Rica, El Salvador was part of the Spanish Empire until all five declared independence in 1821. In 1824, they joined together in the Central American Federation, and all of them flew the same flag with only slight differences until the Federation broke up in 1839. Three of the countries—Honduras, Nicaragua and El Salvador—still have flags similar to the old one flown by the Federation.

The blue in the Salvadorian flag stands for the clear sky, white for peace and harmony. The coat of arms, which appears only on the state flag, is full of symbolism. Its equilateral triangle says that all Salvadorians are equal before the law. Five volcanoes in the triangle represent the five republics in the old Federation, and the Liberty Caps (see page 38) on two of them signify independence. Under the triangle is the national motto: "God, Union and Liberty."

About four-fifths of the 3,000,000 people in El Salvador are either Indians or what Salvadorians call *ladino*—that is, mixed Indian and

European—and the rest are of European descent. Except among the pure Indians, who have kept their own languages, the spoken language is Spanish. Less than half of the people can read or write. *Member, United Nations.*

ETHIOPIA (eeth-ee-OHP-ee-yuh): Part of this ancient country, which the British once called Abyssinia, was known in Biblical times as the Land of Cush. Much of Ethiopia's early history can only be guessed at, and great monuments carved from solid stone are almost all that remain of civilizations that disappeared long ago.

At the time when the rest of Africa was being divided among European rulers, the Empire of Ethiopia fought hard for freedom. It was, in fact, the only important African country which defeated all European invaders in the nineteenth century. Toward the end of the century its national flag was designed. Probably each stripe in the flag was once a separate banner used by one of three different parts of the army. After a time, they were flown one over the other, then finally stitched together. Nobody is quite sure what the colors represent. Some say they stand for the colors of the rainbow; others that they represent faith, hope and charity, the three great Christian virtues.

Today, most Ethiopians are Christians. The Emperor, who heads the official Ethiopian Orthodox Church, traces his ancestry back to King Solomon and the Queen of Sheba. His full title is Conquering Lion of the Tribe of Judah, Elect of God, Emperor of Ethiopia. His emblem, the lion, is perhaps related to the fact that, in the Book of Revelations, Jesus was called the Lion of the Tribe of Judah—the tribe to which Solomon also belonged. The crowned lion appears in the center of the yellow stripe of the state flag. It carries a cross to show that the country

Some of Ethiopia's 750,000 camels.

is officially Christian, although other religions are allowed. The lion does not appear in the national flag.

About one-fifth of the 23,000,000 Ethiopians are Moslems; many follow tribal religions, and there is an ancient sect of Jews. The main language, Amharic, belongs to the same family as ancient Egyptian. Almost all educated Ethiopians speak English, which is taught in many schools. *Member, United Nations.*

FINLAND (FINN-land): Nearly two thousand years ago, bands of hunters and trappers moved into the great forest that covered what is now Finland. For centuries they supplied furs to the traders of Europe, and slowly made clearings for farms around their isolated villages. In the twelfth century, Crusaders from Sweden entered Finland, and before long Sweden ruled the whole country. In the sixteenth century, Sweden's king gave his approval to a national Finnish flag. Its white field stood for the snow of the long winters; the blue in the cross represented the thousands of blue Finnish lakes.

In 1809, the Russian Empire took Finland away from Sweden and ruled over it until 1917. In that year, the czar was overthrown, and Finland received its independence from the new Soviet government in Russia. After using three other flags, the new Republic of Finland in 1920 adopted the flag it had been given long ago by Sweden, making only a slight change. A crown that had been in its center was left out.

About 4,700,000 people live in Finland, most of them Evangelical Lutherans. More than nine-tenths of them speak the Finnish language, which is related to Estonian and Hungarian, but not to any other in Europe. (Its alphabet lacks the letters *b, c, f, w, x* and *z*; the same word stands for both *he* and *she*.) About 350,000 Finns speak Swedish, and both Finnish and Swedish are official languages. There is almost no one in the country who cannot read and write at least one of them. Nearly 2,500 Lapps live in the north. Long ago, these herding people, who apparently came from Asia, gave up their own language and adopted Finnish. *Member, United Nations.*

Young Finnish farmers.

54

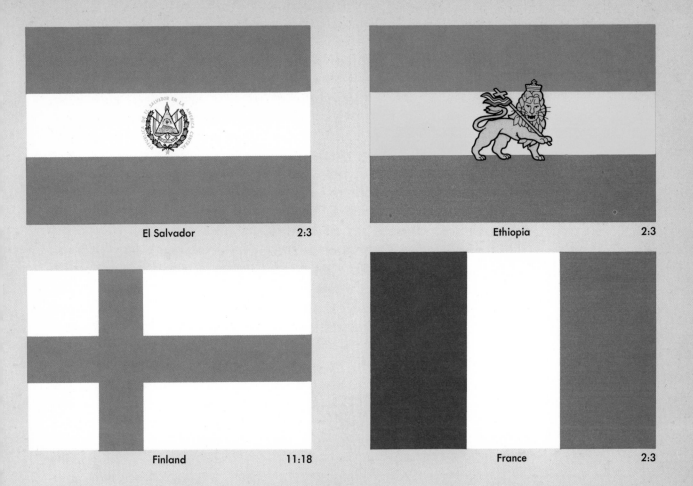

El Salvador 2:3

Ethiopia 2:3

Finland 11:18

France 2:3

FRANCE: Blue, white and red ribbons dangled from the staff of King Charlemagne's banner in the ninth century, and some historians say that these colors have been traditional in France ever since. Certainly King Louis XVI always wore a white decoration on his hat, and the Parisian revolutionaries who opposed him in 1789 took to wearing blue and red—the traditional colors of Paris—on theirs. Hoping to make people feel that he really represented all of France, the king then put the rebel blue and red on *his* hat, next to the royal white. This didn't stop the French Revolution, but later that year, when the rebels won concessions from the king, they kept the blue, white and red as their symbol. In 1790, the new French navy adopted a flag made up of the three colors, the *Tricolor,* and in 1794 it became the national flag. Several times after that, during political upheavals, other flags took its place, but today the flag of the 50,000,000 citizens of the French Republic is again the same Tricolor flown in 1794.

Another very old French symbol is the *fleur-de-lis,* sometimes called in English the "lilies of France." The word *lis* does mean lily, but the unknown artist who first made the design, perhaps in Egypt or India, probably had an iris flower in mind. Before and after Charlemagne,

55

French kings made use of the design, and by the fourteenth century they had become attached to it. The *fleur-de-lis* appeared on the French royal coat of arms when King Edward III of England claimed that the throne of France really belonged to him. To show that he meant what he said, he added the lilies to his own coat of arms in 1340. After that, there was a war between France and England which lasted almost a hundred years. When it was over, the French continued to use their lilies, and the *fleur-de-lis* was still associated with France, even after the country became a republic.

Although France has no official religion, most of its people are Roman Catholics. Only about 2 per cent are Protestants, and there are a few Moslems and Jews. French is the principal language, but around the edges of the country small groups speak other languages—Flemish. Alsatian-German, Italian, Catalan, Basque. In the northwest, some speak Breton, a language related to Welsh. *Member, United Nations.*

United Nations teacher and students during recess, Gabon.

GABON (gah-BAWN): In the fifteenth century, Portuguese ships visited the mouth of the Como River, almost directly on the Equator, along the west coast of Africa. The sailors thought the harbor resembled a certain kind of a coat with a hood—a *gabão,* in Portuguese. So that was what they called the place. Later, their name for the harbor spread to the surrounding country, and the spelling changed to Gabon.

Gabon's great dense forests, with only a few areas of grassy land, were the home of forty tribes that kept their independence until 1885, when France occupied the country. In 1960, it became independent again and adopted a flag with three horizontal stripes. The green stripe stands for the forests, yellow for the sun, and blue for the color of the equatorial sea.

The government of the Gabon Republic says that more than 80 per cent of the people can read and write French, the official language. In addition, there is a separate language for each tribe, including a small group of Pygmies. Long ago, Pygmies were the only inhabitants of the country, but now very few of them remain.

Christian missionaries have made many converts in Gabon. Almost one-third of the half-million Gabonese have become Roman Catholics, and one-tenth are Protestants. About three thousand are Moslems. The rest of the people practice tribal religions. One of the Christian missionaries was the famous advocate of peace, Dr. Albert Schweitzer, who established a hospital deep in the tropical forest and called attention to the need for public health work. *Member, United Nations.*

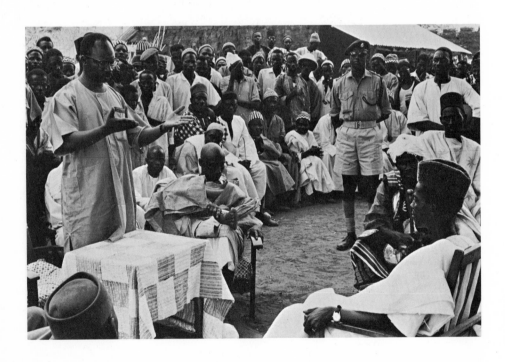

The Prime Minister of Gambia discusses local matters with village leaders.

GAMBIA (GAM-bee-uh): From the fifth to the eighth century, this country (always called *The* Gambia) was part of a great African empire known as Ghana. Then it became part of Songhay, another African empire. In 1455, Portuguese ships looking for slaves explored the Gambia River, and Portuguese settlers began to live along its banks. These settlers intermarried with Gambians.

57

Today, the only indications that Portuguese once lived there are a few names and customs. On Christmas Eve, for example, Christians and Moslems alike take part in a festival that began perhaps five hundred years ago. Men dressed in fantastic naval uniforms parade in the streets, carrying ship models, some as long as twenty feet. These are really gigantic lanterns which have candles inside wooden frames covered with a lacelike paper cut out in elaborate designs. Cherry-colored lanterns hang from the tops of the ships' masts. Paraders also carry models of houses, airplanes and automobiles as part of a celebration that lasts all night.

The British began to trade along the Gambia River in 1588, and the country was made a British colony in 1821. On February 18, 1965, it became independent and adopted its own flag. The red stripe at the top of the flag stands for the sun. The blue is for the Gambia River. Green stands for agricultural resources, and the white stripes are for purity and peace.

There are about 350,000 Gambians belonging to several tribes, each of which keeps its own language. Most are Moslems; a few belong to Christian churches or practice tribal religions. There are about five hundred Europeans in the country, as well as a colony of settlers from Lebanon. English, the official language, is used by the government and in many schools. Children who go to Moslem schools learn Arabic. *Member, United Nations.*

GERMANY, both East and West: In the Middle Ages, all of Europe was made up of many tiny countries called principalities, each one ruled by its own prince or duke or king. As time passed, some of the small states joined together and formed larger countries, such as France and England. The hundreds of small German principalities were grouped together loosely into what was called the Holy Roman Empire. People now say it was neither holy nor Roman nor an empire, because for almost a thousand years princes and the Catholic Popes carried on non-religious squabbles and wars for power; although emperors were crowned, they often did very little ruling, and they were not Romans. At any rate, during those first efforts to unite German-speaking people, the emperors had a flag and a coat of arms in which the colors were red, black and gold.

By 1848, most of the German principalities were still not strongly united under one flag. That year, revolutionists tried to overthrow many of their rulers and form a republic. A man named Carl Schurz was active in this revolt. He later fled to the United States, served as a general in the Union Army during the Civil War, and later became Secretary of the Interior. Two other men, Karl Marx and Friedrich Engels, took part in the 1848 revolution. When it failed, they fled

58

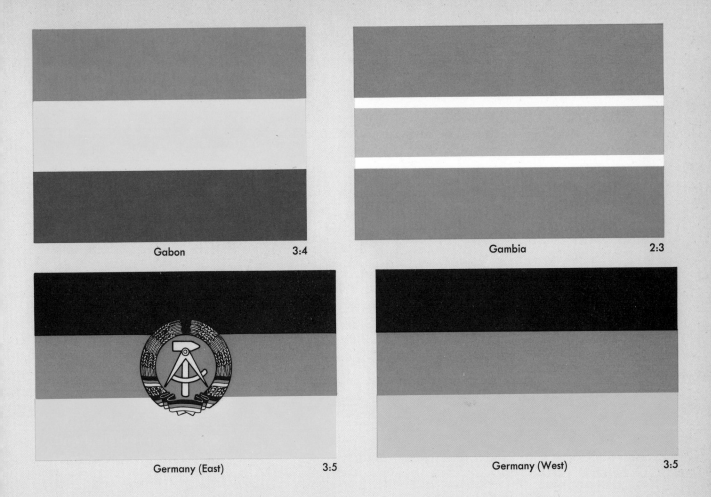

Gabon   3:4

Gambia   2:3

Germany (East)   3:5

Germany (West)   3:5

to England, where they started an international communist revolutionary organization.

The rebels in 1848 adopted the colors that had been in the flag of the old Holy Roman Empire to show that their aim was to unite Germans into one nation. The country was later united—not by the revolutionists, but by an emperor called a kaiser who had his own flag.

After the defeat of Kaiser Wilhelm in World War I, Germany became a republic, and once again the old colors—black, red and gold—made up the flag, which flew over the country from 1918 until Adolf Hitler seized power in 1933.

After Hitler's defeat, Germany was divided into two separate countries. The western part—which had been occupied by the armies of the United States, England and France—became the Federal Republic of Germany. It has a population of nearly 59,000,000, about half Roman Catholic and half Protestant. In 1950, it revived the 1918 flag.

In eastern Germany, which had been occupied by the Soviet army, a socialist country was established. It took the name German Democratic Republic, and in 1950 it, too, adopted the 1918 flag. Nine years later, to avoid confusion, East Germany put a special symbol in the

Each year, West German boys release balloons bearing the message, "All men are brothers." The finders respond with letters.

center of its flag. In this emblem the wreath of grain represents farms, the hammer represents workers, and the pair of compasses stands for industry and science. About 18,000,000 people, 80 per cent of whom are Protestant, live in East Germany.

GHANA (GAH-nuh): From the fourth century A.D. to 1077, when much of Europe was made up of tiny backward countries, a great kingdom stretched across the grassy plains in West Africa. Its name was Ghana, and for some time it had been growing strong because the Ghanaians learned, sooner than their neighbors did, how to make good weapons and tools out of iron. The tools gave them more food and an easier life. The weapons made it possible for kings to build a powerful army. For three hundred years, Ghana's soldiers protected the busy trade routes that crossed the country. Caravans from the north brought in salt to be exchanged for gold that was mined to the south, and every camel or donkey that entered or left Ghana was taxed. The land grew so rich that its ruler's title was King of Gold.

A Moslem army at last defeated the Ghanaians, and in 1077 the empire began to crumble. Finally it died away. But it was not forgotten. On March 6, 1957, when people in Britain's Gold Coast Colony became independent, they called their country Ghana. They liked the name,

60

although the new Republic of Ghana did not occupy any of the same territory as the old empire.

The red in the Ghanaian flag stands for those who worked for independence. The gold is for the country's wealth. Dark green represents the forests and farms, and the black star is the guiding star of African freedom. Until 1966, the head of the government was Kwame Nkrumah, who had been the leader in the fight for independence.

The 17,500,000 Ghanaians belong to eighty-seven different tribes, each with its own tongue. Seven of these are widely spoken, but the official language of the government and of most schools is English. Many of the tribes practice a religion based on veneration of ancestors. There are also a good many Moslems and Christians. *Member, United Nations.*

GREECE: In ancient Greece, each important city was an independent state with its own army. Sometimes an army carried a standard—a long pole with a special emblem at the top. The emblem of Athens was an owl; Thebes had a sphinx, half-woman and half-lion. Long afterward, in the fourteenth century, some Greek cities followed another fashion: they had flags shaped like shields. After 1453, the Turks ruled the country as part of the Ottoman Empire, and for nearly four centuries only the Turkish flag flew in Greece.

In 1821, when the Greeks began a war for independence, they used a flag with a Christian cross on it to show their opposition to the Turks who were Moslems. Some historians think this flag was red and white; others say it was blue and white. It certainly was blue and white after

Ghana: (left) Making cement blocks for a model home; (right) a chief is inaugurated as head of his tribe.

61

Women balancing water jars run a foot race at an age-old Greek festival.

1833. By that time, the Greeks had won independence with the help of Great Britain, France and Russia. Those three countries had chosen a king to rule in Greece—a son of the German King of Bavaria—and blue and white were the colors in his coat of arms. The flag adopted then, with its white cross and nine blue and white stripes, has remained practically unchanged. Greeks now say the blue stands for the sky, and the cross for the Christian faith. The nine stripes may represent the national motto, "Liberty or Death," which in Greek has nine syllables. Or they may symbolize the nine years of war for independence from Turkey. This flag with stripes is only flown at seaports and outside Greece. The flag flown inside the country is all blue, except for the white cross.

Greeks call their country Hellas, and its official name is the Kingdom of Hellas. Its 8,600,000 people speak Greek, which has developed from languages spoken in the city-states of ancient times. The official religion is Greek Orthodox. *Member, United Nations.*

GUATEMALA (gwah-tuh-MAH-luh): More than two thousand years ago, Mayan Indians in this Central American country built roads and cities and a great civilization. After A.D. 900, the cities were deserted and the civilization mysteriously disappeared, but the Indians themselves remained. They were conquered in the sixteenth century by Spaniards who ruled there for the next three hundred years.

In 1821, Guatemala won freedom from Spain in a bloodless revolution. After that, it was part of the Mexican Empire, and then part of

A Guatemalan family at dinner.

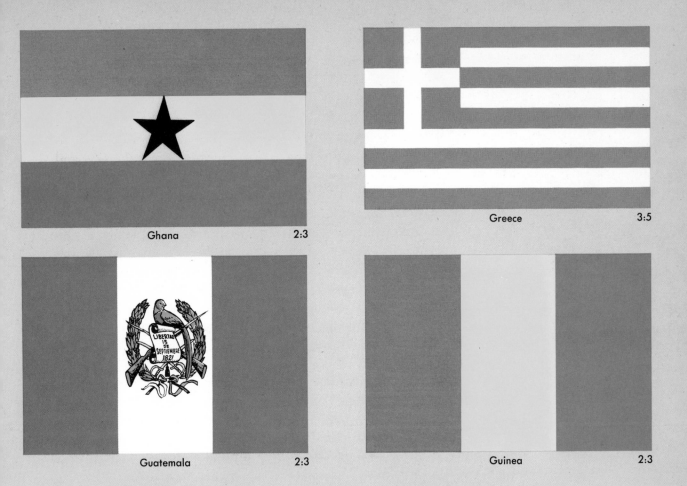

Ghana 2:3

Greece 3:5

Guatemala 2:3

Guinea 2:3

the Central American Federation (see EL SALVADOR). In 1838, it became the independent Republic of Guatemala.

Following a revolution in 1871, the general who led the rebels decreed that the country should have a new national flag. It is still flown today. Its blue stripes represent the desire for perfection, the white stripe its hope for peace. The bird in the coat of arms is the quetzal, a symbol of independence. (The quetzal is also a Guatemalan coin, equal to about one United States dollar.) The scroll in the coat of arms bears the date of the country's independence from Spain.

More than half of Guatemala's 4,500,000 people are pure Indian. Most of them speak their own languages, instead of Spanish, which is used officially. They also keep their traditional religions. A good many Guatemalans are part Spanish and part Indian, and in some cities there are Negroes. The religion of the non-Indians is generally Roman Catholic. *Member, United Nations.*

GUINEA (GHIN-ee): In the fourteenth century a Spanish friar went traveling in many lands, then told what he had seen in a book about the countries of the world and their flags. "The King of Guinea," he wrote, "has a gold flag with a black mountain in the middle. Of Guinea

63

Guinea: (left) a city scene; (right) a country girl of the Fulah tribe.

there is much to say. It contains seven mountains well peopled. . . . They collect the ivory teeth [of elephants] and the gold in the ant-hills which the ants make on the river banks. The ants are as big as cats and dig out much earth."

The author exaggerated a bit, but the fact is that gold still turns up in rich deposits along river banks in this part of Africa. Ants may very well have brought nuggets of it up out of their tunnels. Certainly the country was well peopled, and because it was also easy to reach, it became a favorite hunting ground for European slave traders in the sixteenth century. During the next three centuries, very large numbers of Guineans and their neighbors were captured and sold in the Americas. After the slave trade ended in the nineteenth century, France took control of the country, which had remained independent until then. It regained its independence on October 2, 1958. A month later, the new Republic of Guinea adopted a flag.

Red in the flag stands for blood shed in the struggle for freedom. Green represents the trees and plants of the country. Yellow stands for its sunshine and its gold. There are about 3,500,000 Guineans belonging to a number of different tribes, each with its own language and religious traditions. French is the language used in government and business. *Member, United Nations.*

GUYANA (guy-ANN-uh): In 1581, the Dutch established the first European settlement in the country on the north coast of South America that is now called Guyana. In the next two centuries, the French, Portuguese and British all attempted to take the territory away from the Dutch, and in 1814 the British succeeded. For more than 150 years after that, it was called British Guiana (spelled with *i*, not *y*). Guiana comes from a word in an American Indian language and means "Land of Waters."

The original inhabitants were all American Indians. Today, their

30,000 descendants are called Amerindians, to distinguish them from 325,000 East Indians whose ancestors came from India. More than 200,000 Guyanese are descended from Africans, and there are many others whose ancestors were Chinese or Portuguese. English is the language of government, the schools and most of the people, who number 650,000 altogether.

In preparation for independence, which came May 26, 1966, Guyana's House of Assembly chose a flag which had been designed for them by Whitney Smith, Director of the Flag Research Center in Lexington, Massachusetts. The green in the flag stands for the agriculture and the forests of the country. The golden arrowhead represents mineral wealth. The red triangle stands for the nation-building that lies ahead. A border of white is for water resources and a black border for endurance that will be needed in the future.

Most Guyanese are Hindus, Moslems or Christians. Some of the Amerindians follow their own religions. *Member, United Nations.*

HAITI (HAY-tee): The Republic of Haiti lies in the western third of Hispaniola, an island that Columbus discovered in 1492. The Indians who lived there were willing to be friendly, but they also wanted to be free, and they resisted Spanish rule and religion. Before long, the whole population was wiped out by new diseases that came from Europe.

Wood used by craftsmen comes from Haiti's dwindling forests.

65

By 1697, the Spanish had to surrender to France the part of the island that became Haiti. At that time most of the Haitians were neither Spanish nor French. They were descendants of slaves who had been brought from Africa, and *their* descendants are the majority in Haiti today.

In 1791, the Haitians began to rebel against French rule. In 1804, their revolution succeeded, making Haiti the second country in the Western Hemisphere to win freedom. (The first was the United States.)

During the revolution, one of the Haitian leaders, General Jean Jacques Dessalines, took a French flag and tore out its white stripe. Then he joined together the blue and red stripes to represent, he said, the unity between the black people of pure African ancestry and the lighter-skinned people who had both African and European ancestors. A new national flag was adopted in 1963. Officially, it is a plain design of black and red vertical stripes, but unofficially, most Haitian flags bear the photograph of President Duvalier in the center.

The 4,700,000 people in Haiti speak Creole, a mixture of Spanish, French, Indian and African words. French is the official language of the government and the schools. The religion of the country is Roman Catholic, but many people practice vodun, also called voodoo, which is related to tribal religions from Africa. *Member, United Nations.*

HONDURAS (hon-DURE-us): In Central America, about halfway between North and South America, a finger of land points out into the Caribbean Sea. Here Christopher Columbus stopped in 1502 and claimed for Spain all the country that lay inland. The Spaniards at first called the area Guaymura; later, they gave it the name Honduras, meaning "The Depths." Whoever made the change must have had some special "depths" in mind, but just what they were remains a mystery.

After a revolution in 1821, Honduras joined with four neighboring countries in the Central American Federation. (See EL SALVADOR.) Although the Federation was later dissolved, Honduras kept its blue and white striped flag, but added to the center stripe five stars that stand for the five countries that formed the original union. The middle star represents the Republic of Honduras itself, because it is geographically the middle country.

Most of the 2,300,000 Hondurans are *mestizos*—that is, they have both Spanish and Indian ancestors. A few are pure Indian, or Negro, or Spanish. The Indians of Honduras, unlike those in neighboring countries, have kept very few of their ancient customs or languages. The capital, Tegucigalpa, has an Indian name, but almost everybody speaks Spanish. Their religion is Roman Catholic. Four people out of five have something to do with farming, particularly with the raising and shipping of bananas to the United States. *Member, United Nations.*

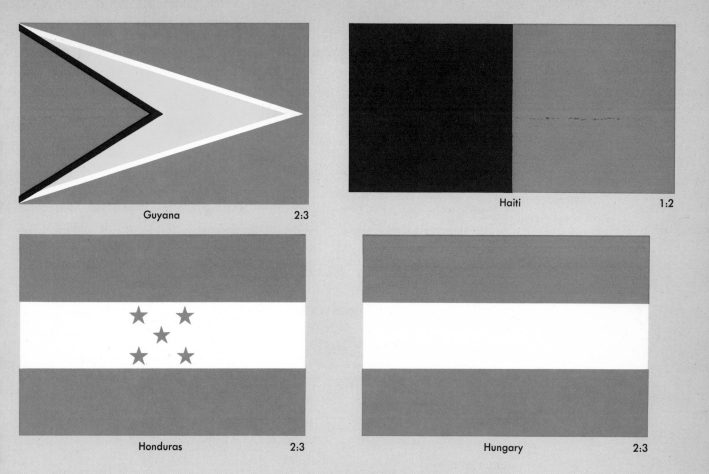

Guyana 2:3

Haiti 1:2

Honduras 2:3

Hungary 2:3

HUNGARY (HUN-gah-ree): The Hungarians are descendants of tribes that came from Asia and settled along the Danube River in the ninth century. The strongest of these tribes was known as the Magyar (MOD-yahr) and today another word for Hungarian is Magyar. When they first reached Europe, the Magyars were wandering horsemen who lived partly by raiding other people. But on the fertile Hungarian land, they turned to farming and settled down. In the centuries that followed, other foreign invaders seized part or all of Hungary at various times, and for a long period it was ruled by Austria. Then in 1869, Hungary was nominally allowed to be the independent and equal partner of Austria, with one monarch for the two countries.

In both world wars, Hungary sided with Germany, and after both wars it lost territory. In 1945, Hungary became a parliamentary republic, and three years later it became the People's Republic of Hungary, ruled by the Communist Party. The government proved to be so dictatorial that in 1956 many of the people rebelled. Troops from the Soviet Union fought against the rebels and helped a different group of communists to take charge of the government. The following year the present red, white and green flag was adopted. It is like earlier flags except that the coat of arms used in 1949 has been removed.

About 10,000,000 people live in Hungary. Two-thirds of those who are religious are Roman Catholic. Most of the rest are Calvinist. Before World War II, there were 770,000 Jews in Hungary, but the Nazis and Hungarian collaborators killed nearly half a million of them.

The Hungarian language is related to Finnish and Estonian and to some languages farther east in the Soviet Union, but it is very different from those spoken in the rest of Europe. However, it does have some words that come from Latin, because until 1840, Latin, the language of the Roman Catholic Church, was also the official language of the government. *Member, United Nations.*

ICELAND (ICE-land): About 1,100 years ago, Norsemen from Norway moved into Iceland, an uninhabited volcanic island that they had found in the North Atlantic Ocean. In A.D. 930, the settlers established a parliament called the *Althing,* which has been in existence ever since. This makes it the oldest parliament in the world.

In 1262, Iceland joined Norway. Then, in 1380, both Norway and Iceland united with Denmark. Norway separated from Denmark in 1814, but Iceland did not. In 1918, Iceland became an independent country, except that she and Denmark shared the same king. Finally, in 1944, Iceland ended the monarchy and became a separate independent republic.

No country in the world has a higher percentage of people who can read and write, and there is one bookstore for every thousand inhabitants. Children can and do read wonderful Icelandic stories, exactly as they were written in the Middle Ages. This is possible because the Icelandic language has changed very little since then.

During the Middle Ages, when the many countries of Europe were fighting exhausting wars, Iceland was at peace. The country still has no army or navy.

The Icelandic flag was adopted in 1916. It has the same design as the flag of Norway, but where the Norwegian flag is red, the Icelandic flag is blue, and vice versa. This in itself says clearly that Iceland is related to Norway, but is also independent. The blue and white have further symbolic meaning, since they are the ancient colors of Iceland, and both the cross and the red stand for ties with Denmark. Almost all of the 187,000 Icelanders are Evangelical Lutherans. *Member, United Nations.*

INDIA (IN-dee-ah): Nearly half a billion people live in this country which is so large that it is almost a continent by itself. Civilization in India goes back a long time. Five thousand years ago, people in the Indus Valley were building cities and using wheeled carts. They also

68

had a form of writing, but nobody has discovered how to read it, so we do not know what language was spoken then.

About half of the inhabitants of India today speak Hindi, the official language. English, as well as Hindi, is much used by the government. About a third of the people speak one of eleven other languages. The remainder belong to smaller groups and speak many languages. Most Indians follow the Hindu religion; about 50,000,000 are Moslems, 11,000,000 are Christians, 8,000,000 are Sikhs, and 3,500,000 are Buddhists.

The flag, adopted in 1947, when India became independent from Britain, tells something of the country's history. In the center is a wheel that has twenty-four spokes, an emblem used by a Buddhist king about 300 B.C. It is also a symbol for peaceful change. Traditionally, the orange stripe stands for the Hindus in India, the green for Moslems, and the white for peace between them. The more recent explanation of the colors is that the orange means honesty and purity; the green stands for courage and man's dependence on the soil; the white for simplicity and peace. The idea of peaceful change was taught by Mohandas Gandhi, who led India to freedom. He persuaded people that they

Village women gather at a new community water hydrant in India.

should disobey Britain's laws—but without violence. These disobedience campaigns were very effective. After World War II, India gained independence, but Gandhi's beliefs did not save him from violence. He was killed by an assassin a few months after India won its freedom. *Member, United Nations.*

INDONESIA (in-doe-NEE-zhya): According to tradition, a simple flag of red and white was used in the past in various parts of this country which consists of three thousand islands. In the seventeenth century the Dutch made many of the islands into a colony. By 1927, Indonesians began to demand independence, and in 1929 the Indonesian National Movement adopted the traditional red and white flag as its own.

During World War II, the Japanese took Indonesia away from the Dutch. Then, in 1945, two days after the surrender of the Japanese, Indonesia declared independence and became the Republic of Indonesia. In the same year, it adopted the red and white flag that had been used by the National Movement—even though it happens to be the same as the one used by Monaco.

A great many different kinds of people make up the Indonesian population. They speak more than thirty different languages, and many of these languages have several dialects. But people from most of the islands can talk to each other in official Indonesian. This language developed out of Malay, the tongue used by traders who went from island to island. About nine-tenths of the 160,000,000 Indonesians are Moslems. Almost all the others are Hindus, Buddhists and Christians, and there are some people who follow tribal religions. *Member, United Nations.*

Indonesian children enjoy an outdoor movie.

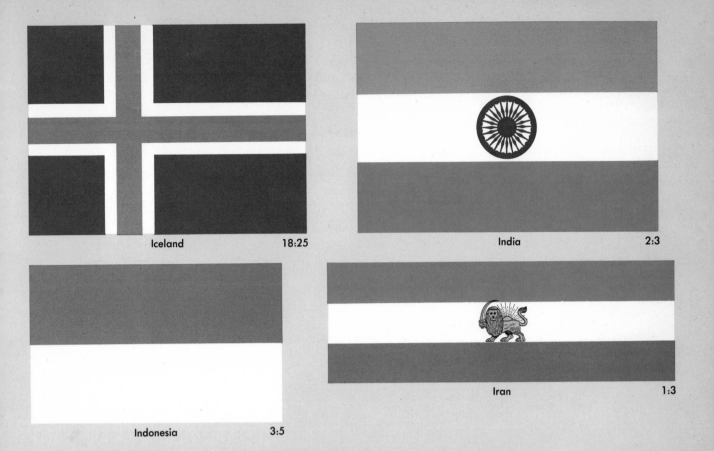

Iceland   18:25

India   2:3

Indonesia   3:5

Iran   1:3

IRAN (eer-ANN): The name *Iran* is related to the word *Aryan*. Aryan tribes lived in southwest Asia 3,500 years ago, and one of them came to be known as the Persian people whose leader, Cyrus the Great, founded a vast empire with headquarters in the land that is now Iran. From then on, almost all Persian kings fought one invader after another. Sometimes they lost; sometimes they won. The country has managed to be more or less independent since 1502. It was still called Persia until 1935, when it became the Empire of Iran, and that same year, a new law gave women almost all of the rights that men have.

The monarch of Iran, called the Shah, rules under a constitution. He must be descended from a shah, and he must be the son of a woman who is both an Iranian and a Moslem. In addition, a shah cannot be crowned until he has a son who is entitled to become shah when he dies.

Iran has had flags for a very long time. The army of Cyrus was said to have carried a white one with a golden crown on it. Rulers often used lions as emblems, not only on flags, but on coins and in decorations for their palaces. No one knows what the lion stood for. Perhaps it was a sacred animal; or it may have been a symbol of power or courage. Sometimes a rising-sun symbol appeared with it. Until the nineteenth century it was usually shown crouching. In 1834, the Shah adopted a flag with a standing lion, a sword grasped in its paw and the sun above its back. The whole emblem symbolizes power, justice

71

and purity. The flag's colors were once white, pale green and soft pink; later, the green was made darker and the pink was changed to red.

About 24,000,000 people live in Iran. Most of them, including several wandering tribes, speak Farsi, also called Persian, the official language of the country. Other tribes speak Turkish or Arabic, and the Gypsies speak Romany. Most of the people are Moslems. There are also Jews, Christians and Zoroastrians. *Member, United Nations.*

Iranian girls, homeward bound after herb-picking.

IRAQ (eer-AK): The oldest human records that scholars have been able to decipher were made about 3100 B.C. in the land of Sumer, which lay between the Tigris and Euphrates Rivers. This river valley now belongs to Iraq; and so no country in the world has a more ancient written history.

After the Sumerians disappeared, Babylonians ruled the land between the rivers. Then came many other rulers, including Assyrians, Persians, Greeks, Romans and Arabs. The Arabs made their capital, Baghdad, a great city of learning in the eighth century. It was there that the stories in the *Arabian Nights* were said to have been collected. Finally the Turks claimed the valley, and it remained part of their empire until Turkey, along with Germany, was defeated in World War I.

After the war, the League of Nations gave Britain responsibility for governing the area of Iraq. The Iraqis elected a king in 1921, and soon afterward he adopted a flag which was very similar to the one used by Jordan, where his brother was ruler. In 1932, the League of Nations recognized Iraq as an independent country. A revolution overthrew the king in 1958 and established the Republic of Iraq, which adopted a new flag. After another revolution in 1963, the flag was changed again. It included three green stars in the middle stripe to indicate the close friendship that existed then between Iraq, Syria and the United Arab Republic. The red in the flag stood for bravery in battle, the white for generosity. Green was a favorite color of the Prophet Mohammed, and the black symbolized the past glories of the Moslem world.

Most of the 8,300,000 Iraqis are Moslems; about 200,000 are Christians. The official language is Arabic. Nearly 1,000,000 people who belong to a tribe of Kurds speak Kurdish; about 150,000 speak Turkish, and 65,000 use either Chaldean or Assyrian. *Member, United Nations.*

Young Kurdish women grinding grain in Iraq.

IRELAND (IRE-land): Much of Ireland was independent until 1601, when English armies finally conquered it. (They had been trying, now and then, for several hundred years.) Irishmen frequently rebelled against England after that, and early in the nineteenth century the rebels began to use a flag that had a white stripe between stripes of green and orange. The white stood for unity between the two kinds of Irishmen who were represented by the other stripes. Green stood for the people in the southern part of the country who were almost all Roman Catholic. Orange was for the northerners, mostly Protestants, who were often called Orangemen. They acquired this name in a roundabout sort of way: originally, they were members of a secret Protestant society who called themselves Orangemen, a name adopted in honor of William III, King of England, who was descended from the royal family of the Netherlands, which in turn was known as the House of Orange.

In 1848, when revolution swept over France, Irish rebels often flew the French blue-and-white-and-red flag alongside their green-white-and-orange one. They often used another flag, too—solid green with a golden harp on it. But during and after a great rebellion, known

Irish children gathering peat for fuel.

as the Rising, in 1916, Irishmen flew only the green-white-and-orange tricolor. It was generally accepted when Southern Ireland finally achieved independence in 1922, and in 1937 it became the official flag of the new republic. Northern Ireland is part of the United Kingdom, along with England, Scotland and Wales.

About 2,600,000 people live in the independent part of Ireland, which is called Eire. English is widely spoken, and all school children must also study Gaelic, the Irish language. *Member, United Nations.*

ISRAEL (IZ-rah-el): In A.D. 70, Romans destroyed the great Temple of the Jews in Jerusalem, and many of the people fled from their homeland. After that, they were often persecuted in the many countries of the world where they settled. During World War II, the Nazis set out to destroy all Jews in Europe and managed to kill 6,000,000 of them. Many who survived wanted a Jewish homeland, and so, after the war, the United Nations called for the formation of a Jewish state in the same area from which their ancestors had originally come.

On May 15, 1948 (in the year 5708, according to the Jewish calendar), the State of Israel was established in what had formerly been called Palestine. Hundreds of thousands of Jews moved to Israel from Europe, America, Africa and Asia, many of them speaking only the language of the country from which they came, others with a knowledge of Hebrew, the ancient language of the Jews. Still others also spoke Yiddish, a language with a curious history. It began in the Middle Ages as a combination of German dialects which Jews continued to use after they fled from persecution in Germany and sought refuge in other countries. Wherever they settled, they borrowed words from the languages spoken around them, and they also added words from Hebrew. Modern Yiddish is written in the Hebrew alphabet.

Many Arabs were already living in the land that became Israel, and Arabic was their language. During a war in June, 1967, Israel occupied large areas in neighboring states. As a result, there may be about as many speakers of Arabic as of Hebrew under Israeli rule. Both languages are official. In addition, 100,000 speak Yiddish and 24,000 speak Ladino (see TURKEY). More than 2,000,000 are Jewish in religion, 55,000 are Druzes and most of the rest are Moslems.

The blue and white stripes of the Israeli flag are those of the prayer shawl that men wear at religious ceremonies. The six-pointed star is known as the Star (or Shield) of David. Nobody can be sure what meaning, if any, it originally had. Certainly it has been an important Jewish symbol in recent times. Archeologists digging in the ruins of the ancient Biblical city of Sidon have excavated a design in the form of this same star. In the fourteenth century it appeared on non-Jewish flags in widely separated places. *Member, United Nations.*

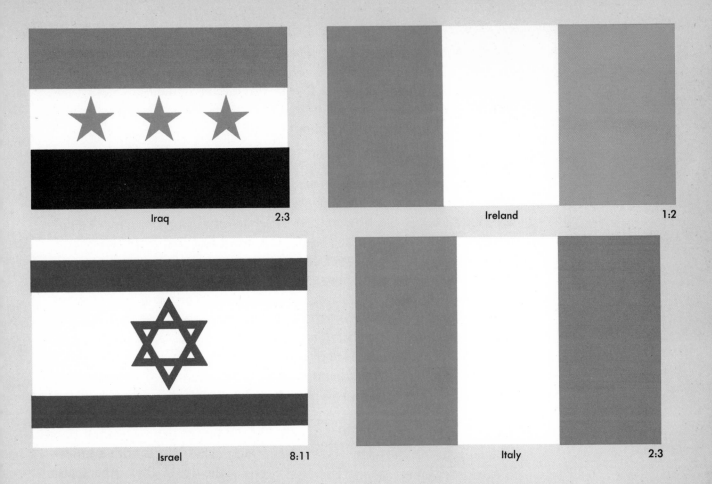

Iraq   2:3

Ireland   1:2

Israel   8:11

Italy   2:3

ITALY (IT-ah-lee): For centuries, Italy was divided into many small separate countries. Although Italians all spoke the same language—and remembered that their ancestors, the Romans, had brought together a great empire—still, they did not have one united government for the whole country. Some of the states were republics. Some were kingdoms. Some were ruled by dukes, others by the Pope, the head of the Roman Catholic Church. Many Italians wished for a united democratic government, and they were encouraged by the revolution in France which began in 1789. Finally, some students in the city of Bologna led a revolt against their king in 1795. They decided to use the blue, white and red flag of the French Republic as the model for their own tricolor flag, but to show that it was truly Italian, they changed the blue stripe to green. The green stands for nature and for man's natural right to be free.

The tricolor became the flag of a republic in northern Italy that lasted a few years, and after that it remained a symbol to all who wanted a single Italian government. It was the flag of Giuseppe Garibaldi, the leader who helped to unify the country in the nineteenth century. In 1861, when Victor Emmanuel II, King of Sardinia, became king of all Italy, he took the revolutionary tricolor as Italy's national flag, but added his coat of arms to the middle of the white stripe. In 1946, after

75

*An Italian stone mason
at work.*

World War II, Italy became a republic, and the coat of arms was removed.

About 53,000,000 people live in the Italian Republic, nearly one-eleventh of them on the island of Sicily. Roman Catholicism is the official religion. *Member, United Nations.*

IVORY COAST: So far as anyone knows, Europeans first visited the Ivory Coast in 1365. They came from France, and France later took control of the land, which was also called Coast of Seeds and Coast of the Good People. On August 7, 1960, the Ivory Coast became an independent country. Its orange, white and green flag is just the reverse of the Irish flag, in which the order of the vertical stripes (from hoist to fly) is green, white and orange.

Soon after independence, the new Republic of Ivory Coast adopted an idea that a great African emperor named Sundiata had found useful seven hundred years before. Sundiata, with a strong army, conquered a large area to the north of the Ivory Coast. Then he put the army to work. Soldiers cleared forests, planted crops, learned how to raise cattle and poultry, and created a rich new farming land. The Ivory

*Ballet class, National
School of Dancing,
Ivory Coast.*

Coast government, too, set its army to work. Soldiers became tractor-driving students, and after clearing new land, they learned how to plant food crops and run poultry farms.

French has remained the official language of the Ivoirians, as the people are called. Each of the country's five main tribal groups has its own language, and each of these has several dialects. Nearly two-thirds of the 3,850,000 people worship tribal gods. About 14 per cent are Christians and 23 per cent are Moslems. *Member, United Nations.*

JAMAICA (juh-MAY-kuh): When Christopher Columbus discovered this island in 1494, Arawak Indians farmed and fished near the shore and hunted in the high Blue Mountains. The last of the Arawaks died or were killed while Jamaica was a Spanish colony. In 1655, the British captured the island and for many years it was a headquarters for pirates. British rule lasted until 1962. Then the island became independent with a parliamentary form of government.

The black in Jamaica's flag stands for hardships, partly overcome but partly still to be faced. Gold is for natural wealth and the beauty of sunlight. Green is for hope and agricultural resources. Taken all together, the flag means this: "Hardships there are, but the land is green and the sun shines."

Many of the 2,000,000 Jamaicans are descended from African slaves. Settlers have also come from Europe, India and China, and there has been much intermarriage between Jamaicans of different origins. The country's motto is "Out of many, one people." Some Jamaicans practice a form of the ancient African religions; about one-half are Protestants. English is the language of the schools, and many people also use their own dialect of English. *Member, United Nations.*

JAPAN: More than three hundred years ago, the most powerful men in Japan were members of a warrior family named Tokugawa. The head of the family, whose title was *shogun,* had more authority than the emperor himself. Early in the seventeenth century the Tokugawa shoguns began to fear that Japan might change; foreigners might upset traditions—even persuade their subjects to revolt. So, in 1637, they forbade all outsiders to enter the country. The only exceptions were a few Chinese and some Dutch businessmen and sailors. The shogun welcomed the Dutch because they brought knowledge of what was happening in Europe and America, and everything the Japanese learned from them was called "the Dutch teaching."

Shoguns kept their island secluded from the world until 1853, when a United States naval officer, Commodore Matthew C. Perry, visited Japan in a warship. The Japanese studied the vessel and decided there was only one way to keep Westerners from invading their country:

A Japanese wedding ceremony.

they would have to build modern machines and factories and make modern ships and weapons for themselves. But first they must send their own people to learn Western skills.

Many Japanese soon came to believe that they would do better without the Tokugawa shogun. In 1867, he gave up his power and allowed the emperor to become the real ruler. The emperor, who was only fifteen years old when he came to the throne, called himself Meiji (pronounced MAY-jee), and his reign is known as the Meiji Restoration.

In 1870, Japan adopted a national flag. The red circle in the center represents the sun, which has long had special meaning for the Japanese people. According to traditional beliefs, their island was created by the sun goddess, and they are her descendants.

Most of Japan's 98,300,000 people are believers in Shinto, an ancient faith that was originally based on the worship of the emperor's ancestors. Shinto has now become mostly a set of rules for conduct, and almost half of its followers combine it with Buddhist teachings. There are about half a million Japanese Christians. About 15,000 white-skinned tribesmen, called Ainus, live in the northernmost part of Japan. They do not resemble the Japanese and their language is not related to any other in the world. They also have their own religion in which the worship of bears is important. *Member, United Nations.*

78

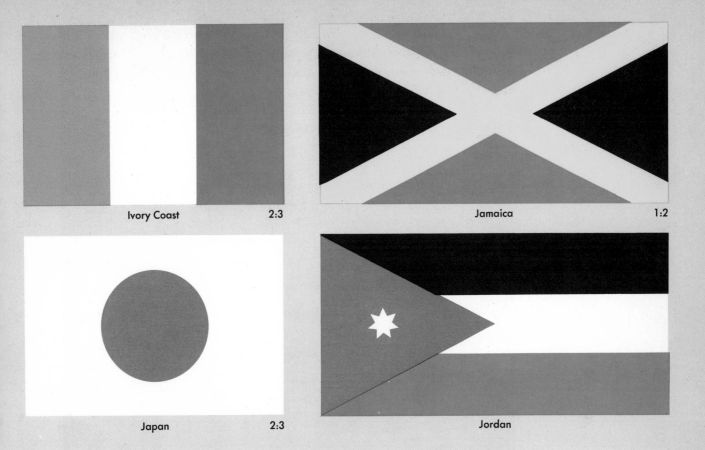

Ivory Coast   2:3

Jamaica   1:2

Japan   2:3

Jordan

JORDAN (JOR-dun): Between the First and Second World Wars, Britain ruled an area called Palestine that had belonged to the Turkish Empire. After the end of World War II, the western part of Palestine became the Jewish State of Israel. The eastern part, which had been called Transjordan, became the independent country of Jordan. Many Arabs from the Israeli section of Palestine moved to Jordan, and the population of that country rose to 2,000,000. In a war in June, 1967, Israel occupied part of Jordan, and Arabs from this area fled into the unoccupied portion. By 1968 there were altogether about 600,000 Arab refugees in Jordanian-controlled territory.

The colors of Jordan's flag have deep meaning for Moslems, not only inside the country, but wherever Arabic is spoken. Black, white and green stand for three families that were very important in early Islamic history (see page 10). And red, which has long been a Moslem color, now stands for the revolt against Turkey in 1916. The seven-pointed star represents seven verses of the Koran, the holy Moslem Book.

Jordan came by its flag in the following way: in 1916, during World War I, Arabs who lived along the eastern shore of the Red Sea broke free from the control of Turkey and established an independent country called the Hejaz. A leader named Hussein became king, and he adopted a flag that had a red triangle at the hoist and three horizontal

79

stripes, black over green over white. In 1921, King Hussein's son Abdullah was made emir of British-ruled Transjordan and adopted his father's flag with certain changes. He put a white seven-pointed star in the red triangle and switched the positions of the white and green stripes. Finally, in 1946, when Transjordan received independence, it changed its name to the Hashemite Kingdom of Jordan (Hashem was the name of the royal family) and retained the 1921 flag. Meanwhile, the Hejaz, from which the design had come in the first place, had been annexed by Saudi Arabia and no longer flew a flag of its own. *Member, United Nations.*

A local artist explains his work at an art show in Amman, capital of Jordan.

KENYA (KENN-yuh): In the eighth century A.D., Arab merchants began trading in the part of East Africa that is now Kenya. The Portuguese explorer Vasco da Gama arrived there in the fifteenth century. For a long time after that, Arabs and Portuguese fought against each other and against the Kenyans, many of whom they seized and sold as slaves. Finally, toward the end of the nineteenth century, Britain gained control of the land.

In 1953, a Kenyan organization known as the Mau Mau began a ferocious struggle against the British, who responded by jailing 60,000 Kenyans, including Jomo Kenyatta, leader of the revolution. When independence was won in 1963, Kenyatta became Prime Minister of the Republic of Kenya. His new government adopted a flag that has a big African shield in its center. Behind the shield are crossed spears called *assegais*.

The Africans in Kenya belong to about fifty tribes, of which the largest is the Kikuyu. When members of two different tribes want to talk to each other, they speak Swahili, an international tongue used in much of Africa. English is the official language of the government, and both English and Swahili are taught in schools.

More than one-third of the Africans follow tribal religions; about half are Christians and about 4 per cent are Moslems. Among the non-Africans there are about 150,000 Asians, partly Moslem, partly Hindu; and about 50,000 Europeans, mostly British Christians. *Member, United Nations.*

KOREA (koh-REE-ah), both South and North: For many centuries the emperors of Korea would not let foreigners enter the country, and Koreans could not travel abroad. Then, late in the 1800's, Emperor Kojong made changes. Korea stopped being the Hermit Kingdom and began to trade with other countries. For the first time it felt the need for a flag. Government officials collected designs from which the Emperor chose one that became official.

The background was white, which stands for peace. (Koreans are so fond of white that they are often called "the White-clad People.") The circle in the center, divided by an S-shaped line, is called the Yin-Yang symbol and represents many things. First of all, it symbolizes the idea that there are two sides to everything — good and evil, male and female, night and day, and so on. The red half of the circle stands for the sun, the blue half for the moon. The designs made of black bars are called Divine Designs. They, too, are full of meaning. For example, long bars outside short bars mean that those who are stronger should protect those who are weaker. Short bars outside a long bar mean that the one who is most precious (the long bar) should be protected by those who are less important (the short ones). The symbolism in this flag is practically endless, and Koreans say it is supposed to make people think about the meaning of the whole universe. The design itself was based on four ancient religious principles.

The Kingdom of Korea flew such a flag until the country was seized as a colony of Japan in 1910. During World War II, Britain, the United States, China and the Soviet Union agreed that Korea should be independent after the war. Then, by agreement among them, Soviet troops occupied the northern part of the country and United States troops occupied the southern part. In May, 1948, the Republic of Korea was

"Just married!"—124 Christian couples after a mass wedding in South Korea.

formed in South Korea and adopted the flag of the Kingdom of Korea, but made a slight change in the shapes of the red and blue areas and in the position of the Divine Designs.

In the same month, the People's Democratic Republic of Korea was formed in North Korea and adopted a separate flag which included the five-pointed star that appears on flags of several countries governed by communists.

About 28,000,000 people live in South Korea. About 12,000,000 live in North Korea. Many are Confucians, Buddhists, Christians and believers in the Chondogyo religion. The language is Korean.

82

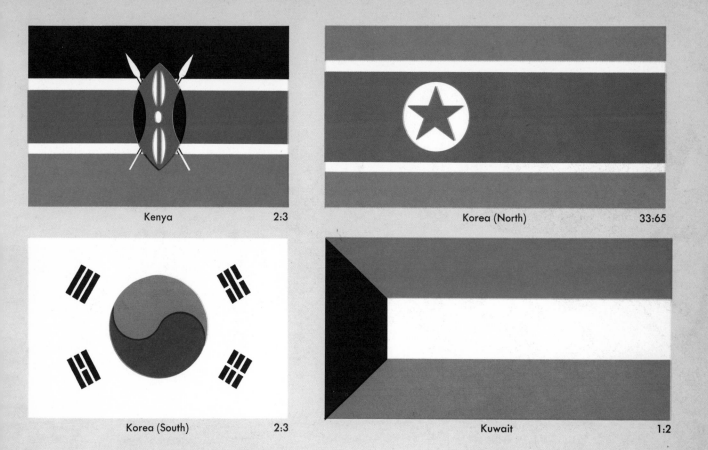

Kenya   2:3

Korea (North)   33:65

Korea (South)   2:3

Kuwait   1:2

KUWAIT (koo-WITE): About three hundred years ago, people from central Arabia settled along the shore at the head of the Persian Gulf, where they became fishermen, shipbuilders and merchants. The small Moslem state of Kuwait developed from these settlements. In 1899, Britain began to direct its foreign affairs.

In 1945, a rich oil field was discovered in Kuwait, and immense wealth poured in. Life for most Kuwaitis began to change. The government now says that its 470,000 citizens have the highest average incomes in the world. Although this doesn't mean that all Kuwaitis share equally in the wealth, a great deal of money goes into things that benefit most of the people. Medical care is free. So is education. By 1965, about 60 per cent of the people could read and write Arabic, the official language. School children are given not only books, but also meals and clothes. If young people want to go on to college in foreign countries, the government pays their expenses. Water, on the other hand, still costs money in this desert land. Many people must buy it from drivers of tank trucks who charge by the gallon for pumping it into containers on the roofs of homes.

When the State of Kuwait became independent in 1961, its ruler, the Emir, decreed a new flag. The red stripe stands for traditional horsemanship and swordsmanship; black is for bravery in war, white for the

83

Learning engine repair at an oil company's training center, Kuwait.

great achievements of so small a country. The green symbolizes the wish for growing things. And that wish may very well come true. Part of the national income has gone into building a huge plant that is changing sea water into fresh water for irrigation. *Member, United Nations.*

LAOS (LOUZ): The Kingdom of Laos was founded in the thirteenth century and was once called Lanxang, which means "Land of a Million Elephants." In 1893, France made Laos into part of the French colonial system. By 1954, the Laotians had regained full independence and were governed by a constitutional monarch.

No census has ever been taken in Laos, but its people probably number between 2,500,000 and 3,000,000. About half speak either Lao, the official language, or Thai; the two are closely related. These people are Buddhists and they arrange their lives according to a calendar based on the cycles of the moon. The other half of the people belong to tribes that speak various languages and have their own traditional religions. One of the tribes grows and exports a good deal of

84

A Buddhist monk, Laos.

opium. Only about one-fifth of the Laotians can read or write, but the majority can play at least one musical instrument.

According to the Laotian government, the three-headed elephant on the flag stands for three parts of the ancient Laotian kingdom united into one. The white parasol over the elephant is a symbol of monarchy. The five steps under it stand for the first five commandments of Buddhism: do not kill; do not steal; do not lie; do not covet thy neighbor's wife; do not abuse the use of liquor. *Member, United Nations.*

LEBANON (LEB-uh-nun): For a long time before World War I, this country was ruled by Turkey. Then France supervised its government for a number of years. In 1943, Lebanese patriots designed a flag that their country could use as soon as it was free. Independence came in 1944.

The red in the flag stands for sacrifice, the white for peace. The tree in the center, symbolizing strength, holiness and eternity, is the cedar of Lebanon, which has been famous around the Mediterranean Sea for nearly five thousand years. The huge logs went to Egypt in ships sent by the pharaohs, who wanted them for beams in their buildings. King Solomon, according to the Bible, had "fourscore thousand hewers in the mountains," cutting the trees to build his temple in Jerusalem. But at last there were almost none to carry away. The great forests of Lebanon had been destroyed and the hills left bare. Only a few of the cedars have survived, and they are now protected by the Lebanese government. No one may cut them without permission.

In this land of about 2,300,000 people, the language is Arabic. The president of the Republic of Lebanon must be a Christian and the prime minister a Moslem. This reflects the division of the population, half and half between the two religions. *Member, United Nations.*

LESOTHO (leh-soo-too): This small kingdom, formerly the British protectorate of Basutoland, gained full independence in October, 1966. The white in the flag it adopted symbolizes peace. Green stands for the country itself; blue for the sky and for rain; red for faith and prayer. The white design on the flag is a straw hat — one of the thirty different kinds traditionally worn by the people.

Lesotho has also adopted official spellings and forms for words that varied a good deal in the past. The proper term for citizens of the country is Basotho. The same word is also used as an adjective — the Basotho constitution, for example. The language is Sesotho.

Lesotho owes its existence as a nation very largely to the efforts of one man, a great Basotho chieftain named Moshoeshoe (pronounced mosh-WESH-way). Early in the nineteenth century, Moshoeshoe united a number of tribes who had been attacked by Zulu soldiers and led them to the place that is now Lesotho. Here he established a kingdom and fought off the Zulus. Most of the people who joined him spoke Sesotho. It is still the main language of the country, although English is used officially by the government.

After Moshoeshoe had pushed the Zulus back, he had to face another danger. Farmers of Dutch descent, known as Boers, came from the Cape Colony of South Africa and tried to take the land away from the Basotho. Moshoeshoe fought with the Dutch and asked Great Britain to protect his country. In 1843, the British made it a protectorate, but changed their minds six years later and withdrew. This forced the Basotho to fight once again for their land. Finally, to keep peace, Britain in 1868 made Moshoeshoe's kingdom part of the British Empire, and it remained under British control until 1966.

Most of Lesotho's 860,000 people are Africans. There are a few Europeans and Asians and a few of mixed parentage. About half follow Christian religions and half worship traditional gods. *Member, United Nations.*

Laos   2:3

Lebanon   2:3

Lesotho   2:3

Liberia   10:19

LIBERIA (lie-BEER-ee-uh): In 1817, a group of white men and women in the United States had the idea that slave owners would be encouraged to free their slaves if the freedmen could go to live in a country of their own. So an organization, the American Colonization Society, was formed to collect money and buy land in West Africa. A few freed slaves agreed to be colonists, and in 1822 they sailed for the new country which had been named Liberia.

The plan did not appeal to very many free Negroes. Only about three thousand went to Liberia in the next twenty-five years. Nor did slave owners cooperate as they had been expected to do, and in 1847 the American Colonization Society gave up altogether. Under the leadership of Joseph J. Roberts the colony declared independence, and Roberts became Liberia's first president. A committee of women designed its first flag, which reflected both the country's American origin and its own identity. The eleven stripes stand for the eleven signers of the Liberian Declaration of Independence. The single white star represents the country itself, for it was the only Negro republic in Africa at that time. The red stands for bravery and valor and reminds Liberians of the courage of the American Negroes who were their country's founders. White is for purity, and the dark blue represents what was called at that time the "Dark Continent of Africa."

A village market, Liberia.

The Republic of Liberia today has about 1,070,000 people. Some of them are descendants of American Negroes; many are aborigines — that is, native Africans whose ancestors lived in the area before the Americans came. Only persons of African descent, including American Negroes, may become Liberian citizens, and only citizens may own real estate.

Most of the people near the coast are Christians; a number of tribes in the interior keep the Moslem and tribal beliefs they had before the colony was started. English is the official language, and a number of tribal languages are widely used. *Member, United Nations.*

LIBYA (LIB-ee-uh): This North African country, which is larger than Alaska, has been claimed by one invader after another for more than two thousand years. First came the Phoenicians, then the Romans, and later, Arabs swept over the land. The Turks ruled there for a long time, then finally the Italians, when Benito Mussolini was dictator, not long before World War II. After the war, Libya was the first colonial territory to receive full independence under a plan worked out by the United Nations. It became a constitutional monarchy in 1951 when its National Assembly elected a king who had been both a political and a religious leader.

Most of the 1,650,000 people are Moslems, but there are Jewish, Catholic and Eastern Orthodox Libyans, too. Each religious group has schools of its own, and there are public schools, but only about 40 per

88

cent of the people have learned to read and write. Arabic is the language of the country.

When the United Kingdom of Libya adopted a constitution, it also chose a flag. The red stripe stands for blood shed in battle and also for Fezzan, one of the country's three traditional regions. Green represents farming and the former province of Tripolitania. Black stands for battles of the past, for Cyrenaica and for the Senussi group of Moslem leaders. The crescent is a Moslem symbol, and the five-pointed star represents hope, belief in God and love of country. *Member, United Nations.*

Students learn typewriting in UNESCO school, Libya.

LIECHTENSTEIN (LEEKH-ten-shtine): For a long time the Principality of Liechtenstein, which lies between Switzerland and Austria, was dependent on either Austria or Germany, but it remained neutral in World War I, and at the end of the war declared its complete independence. It was neutral again during World War II.

Liechtenstein has an area of only 62 square miles and a population of only 18,000. Because it would be too costly for this small country to send ambassadors to other countries, it has arranged to have Switzerland represent it. The language of the country is German and the people are Roman Catholic.

The blue and red flag of Liechtenstein is made in two different styles —one to hang vertically and the other to hang horizontally, like most other flags. In each kind, the crown is placed so that its top is pointing upward.

LUXEMBOURG (LUX-em-burg): In A.D. 963 a French prince built a fortress called Lucilinburhuc on a rocky hill in the midst of the lands he controlled. That was the beginning of the country now called the Grand Duchy of Luxembourg. In the thirteenth century, some of the rulers of Luxembourg used the colors red, white and blue in their coats of arms, and those are the colors of the flag today.

At times during its long history, Luxembourg was independent, but it was often ruled by powerful neighbors and did not fly a flag of its own. When, in 1839, the Grand Duchy began to move toward independence, the question of a new flag came up. The three traditional colors were chosen and arranged with a horizontal red stripe at the top, then a blue stripe, then a white. Several years passed before anyone noticed that this arrangement broke an ancient tradition of flag-making: the white should have been placed between the two other colors. So the white stripe was shifted, even though the change gave the Luxemburgers a flag almost like the flag of the Netherlands. The Luxembourg blue is supposed to be lighter and the whole flag is longer than the Dutch flag.

Luxembourg is a constitutional monarchy. Most of its 320,000

89

Traditional springtime dancing procession, Luxembourg.

people are Roman Catholics. The official languages, French and German, are taught in schools and so is the national language, Luxembourgeois, also called Letzeburgesch. *Member, United Nations.*

MALAGASY (mal-uh-GAHS-ee) **REPUBLIC:** Long ago, perhaps about 250 B.C., olive-skinned people who may have come from Indonesia settled in Madagascar, which is the fourth largest island in the world. At a different time, dark-skinned people moved onto Madagascar from Africa. Later, Arabs arrived. About 1810, the French and British began to compete with each other for control of the island, and by 1855 the French had won out. They ruled the island until 1960, when it became the Malagasy Republic.

After the new government was organized, it announced a contest for the design of a national flag. In the winning design, based on the flag of a people called Hovas who once ruled Madagascar, the white stripe stands for purity, the red for independence and the green for hope. The 6,300,000 Malagasy speak a language related to the languages of Malaysia, but French is taught in the schools. About 1,000,-000 Malagasy are Catholics; the same number are Protestants. The rest follow the ancient religions of the people which are based on the worship of dead ancestors. Funerals are very important and tombs are sometimes very elaborate. *Member, United Nations.*

90

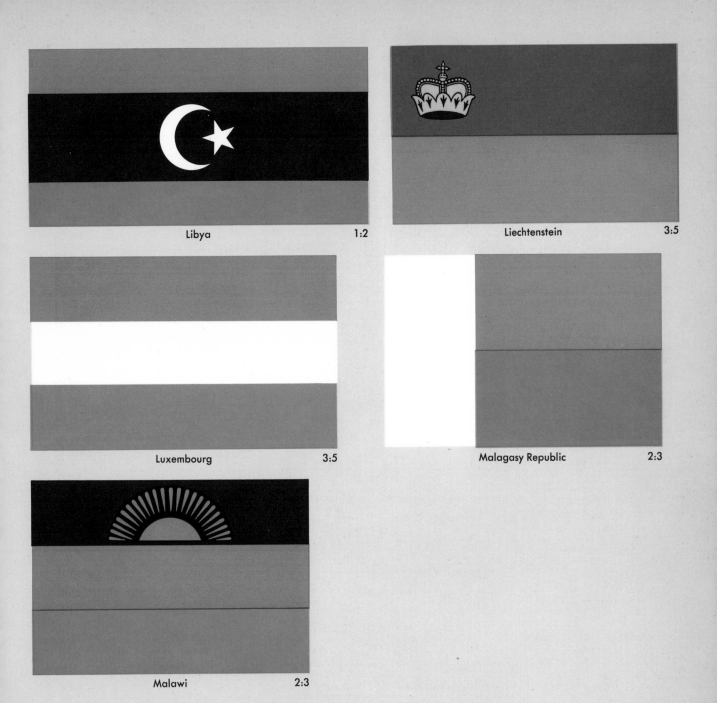

Libya 1:2

Liechtenstein 3:5

Luxembourg 3:5

Malagasy Republic 2:3

Malawi 2:3

MALAWI (mal-LAH-wee): In 1859, the British explorer-missionary
David Livingstone made a journey inland from the east coast of Africa
to Lake Nyasa, a deep body of water bordered by high mountains on
the west. He was the first European to visit the country that later became
a British colony called Nyasaland, but the people who lived there were
already well known to other foreigners — the Arab slave traders who
often swept down on them from the upper end of the lake. After 1891,
the British began to end the raids and to rule over various tribes in a
five-hundred-mile strip along the lake shore.

91

In July, 1964, Nyasaland became an independent republic, adopted the name Malawi and chose a flag. The black in the flag stands for all Africans. The rising sun represents the dawn of hope and liberty in Africa. Red is for the blood of Africans who have given their lives for freedom. Green is for the vegetation which stays green the year round.

About 3,900,000 of Malawi's people are Africans; 12,000 come from India and 8,000 are Europeans. The Africans belong to several related Bantu tribes, and most of them follow tribal religions and speak their own languages. Many Malawians rely on Swahili as an intertribal tongue. Several of their languages are used in radio broadcasts, but English is official. *Member, United Nations.*

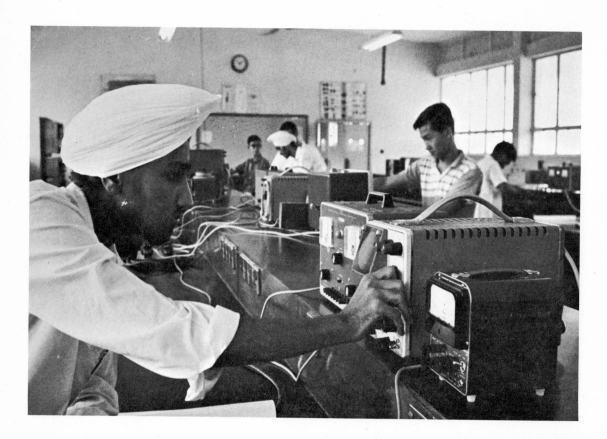

Electrical engineering students, Malaysia.

MALAYSIA (mah-LAY-zhya): More than 40,000 years ago, primitive men lived in caves on the island of Borneo, part of which is in Malaysia, and some primitive tribes still live there today, practicing their ancient tribal customs and religions. Most Malaysians, however, follow one of the principal world religions. The first of these to reach Malaysia was Buddhism, and the first important kings in the area were Buddhist. A Hindu empire developed later. Then, in the fourteenth century, Arab traders arrived, bringing Islam. Britain began to rule the Malay Peninsula early in the nineteenth century, and at that time large numbers of people from India and China moved in, bringing their religions and customs with them.

Throughout the peninsula and on neighboring islands, there were many separate British colonies until, in 1957, eleven of them united to become states in the Federation of Malaya. In most of these states, hereditary sultans had ruled under the British. All eleven, plus three others, united in 1963 to form a new country called Malaysia, and they elected a king.

The flag of Malaysia was based on the flag that had been used by Malaya, largest of the fourteen members of the Federation. There are fourteen stripes, one for each of the former colonies. The star has fourteen points, and it is yellow—a symbol of royalty. The crescent stands for the religion of the Malay part of the population, which is Moslem. The blue symbolizes unity.

Although many languages are spoken in Malaysia, most people can talk to each other in Malay, which according to the constitution had to become the official language of the country in 1967. English is also taught in the schools. The majority of the 9,000,000 Malaysians are Malays and related peoples; about one-third are of Chinese origin; the rest came from India, Pakistan and other countries. In 1965, Singapore, one of the fourteen states of Malaysia, seceded and became a separate country. *Member, United Nations.*

MALDIVE (MAL-dive) **ISLANDS:** Long ago, people from the island of Ceylon sailed more than four hundred miles into the Indian Ocean and settled on some of the tiny coral Maldive Islands. The Maldivians were Buddhists until 1153, when they were persuaded to become Moslems. Portuguese captured the islands in the sixteenth century, but were finally driven out, and the people remained independent until 1887. Then they became part of the British colonial system. In 1965, they regained their independence under the rule of a sultan.

The language of the 97,000 Maldivians is related to Sinhalese, which is spoken by part of the people of Ceylon. English is also much used and studied in schools, including schools for girls which were recently started.

Through most of the eight hundred years after Maldivians were converted to the Islamic faith, their flag was pure red with no design on it. Then a prime minister, who has been called the Mussolini of the Maldives, changed the flag to its present form. He did this, it is said, because he thought red had become associated with communism. The red in the new flag stands for the blood the Maldivians shed to win freedom. Green is for peace and prosperity, and the crescent is a Moslem emblem. At first, the flag had a vertical stripe at the hoist (it was made of alternating diagonal bands of black and white), but the stripe was expensive to manufacture and is no longer used. *Member, United Nations.*

MALI (MAH-lee): A vigorous empire called Mali developed in West Africa in the thirteenth century. For two hundred years it brought prosperity and abundance to a large area, although its rulers often used force to maintain their power and to protect themselves from outsiders. In one of the cities, Timbuktu, scholars built a university that was famous all over Africa and Europe.

In the fifteenth century, another empire known as Songhai replaced Mali and lasted until Moslem armies from the north destroyed it in the sixteenth century (see NIGER). In the nineteenth century, the French invaded the country and made it part of a colony known as French Sudan. Finally, in 1960, independence came. The new country took the name Republic of Mali and began to conduct its business as a partially socialist democracy.

In 1961, Mali adopted a flag based on one it had used briefly while it was in a federation with Senegal (see SENEGAL). Its yellow stripe stands for purity and the country's natural resources. Red is for courage and blood shed in the fight for independence. Green is for the vegetation in this largely agricultural land.

Most of the 4,600,000 Malians are Moslems. They belong to many different tribes and speak many languages. One important language, Bambara, now has an alphabet and can be written, as can several others. The official language of the whole country is French, which is also used in schools. *Member, United Nations.*

Girls on their way home from school, Mali.

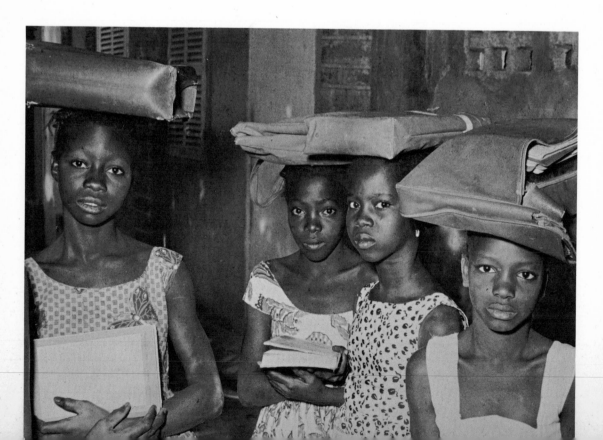

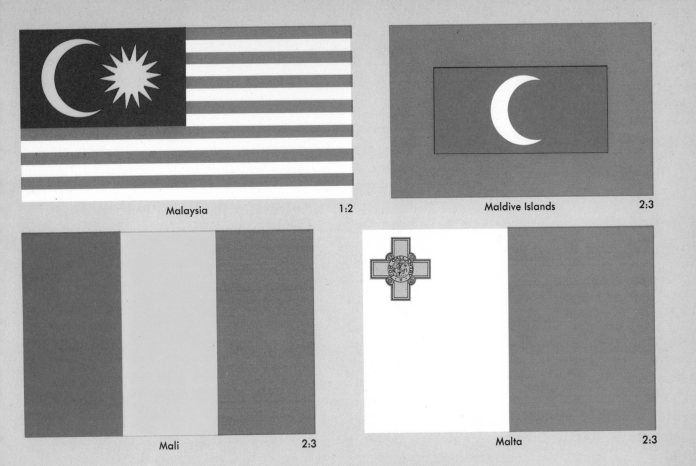

Malaysia 1:2

Maldive Islands 2:3

Mali 2:3

Malta 2:3

MALTA (MAWL-tuh): This island in the Mediterranean Sea has been ruled by Phoenicians, Greeks, Romans, Carthaginians, Arabs, Sicilians, French and English. According to tradition, Count Roger, a Crusader from Normandy, landed on Malta in 1094 to drive out the Arabs. The Maltese welcomed Roger, and he rewarded them by allowing them to use in their flag the white and red colors of his coat of arms.

From 1530 to 1798, Malta was an independent country ruled by a Christian military organization sometimes called the Knights of Malta. Then the French general Napoleon took the island away from the Knights, and the British took it from Napoleon in 1802 and annexed it in 1814.

During World War II, Malta held out against strong German bombing, and Britain's King George VI awarded the Cross of St. George to the island for the heroism of its people. This honor gives anyone who receives it the right to add to his name the letters G.C. (George Cross). That is why the name of the island is sometimes written Malta, G.C. When Malta achieved independence in 1964, the cross was placed on the flag, which has the red and white colors supposedly going back to the year 1094. The cross on the flag is not the same as a Maltese Cross, which looks like the one shown on the left.

The 325,000 Maltese speak their own language, based on the Semitic languages of the Arabs and of the ancient Carthaginians, with many Italian words added. Children in the elementary grades are taught in Maltese. In the last years of high school they study English, and they use English in the university. The government conducts its business in both Maltese and English, but Maltese is the official language. Most Maltese are Roman Catholics. *Member, United Nations.*

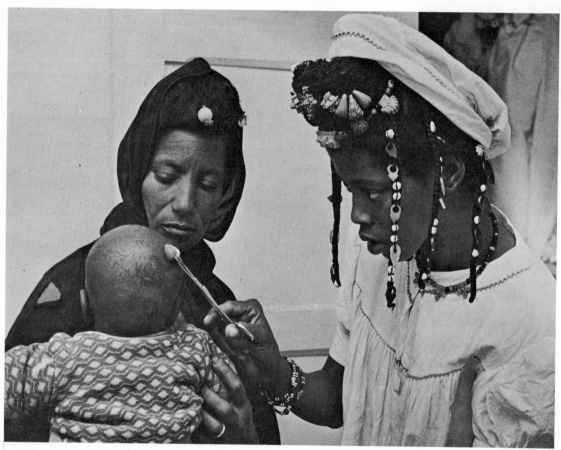

Nurse teaching child care, Mauritania.

MAURITANIA (mor-uh-TAIN-yuh): In the third century, Arabs began finding their way into the Sahara Desert to trade with nomadic Berbers who lived there. When the Arabs became Moslems, they brought their new religion with them and converted the Berbers. Over the years the two peoples mingled and became one, known as the Moors. Their home-land was Mauritania, which means "country of the Moors." By the middle of the eleventh century the Moors had developed a special crusading form of the Islamic faith which they set out to spread by military force. First they conquered all of northwest Africa. Then they

96

swept on into Spain, where Moslems were already in power. The Moors with their very strict religion ruled there for three centuries before Christians drove them out.

Meanwhile, tribes of Moors had still been living in Mauritania. Those who came back from Spain joined them, and they remained independent until the French conquered them in the nineteenth century.

In 1958, when Mauritania won the right to govern itself, its leaders adopted a flag made up of symbols often associated with Islam — the star, crescent and the color green, which also stands for prosperity and hope. In 1960, the country gained full independence and took the name Islamic Republic of Mauritania.

Mauritanians who have Negro ancestors now live peacefully with descendants of the early Moors. They number about 1,000,000 altogether, and most of them make their living as farmers or fishermen. The government believes that many will become industrial workers when their country begins to use its iron ore deposits, which are very large. Three-fourths of the Mauritanians can read and write, according to government figures. Arabic is the language of the people, but French is used by the government. *Member, United Nations.*

MEXICO (MEK-sih-koh): The Mexicans like to tell a story about a poor wandering band of Indians whose medicine men long ago made a prophecy: somewhere, the tribe would see an eagle perched on a cactus and holding a snake in its claws. There, said the medicine men, the band should make its permanent home. In the Valley of Mexico the wanderers did see such a sight on an island in a lake. They settled on the island in A.D. 1325, built a city, and founded the Aztec empire that dominated other tribes in much of Mexico.

Invaders came from Spain between 1519 and 1521, conquered the Aztecs and ruled all of Mexico for the next three hundred years. By 1821, when the Mexicans declared independence from Spain, they were governing a territory which included a large strip of the continent north of the present Mexican border. This northern area had begun to attract frontiersmen from the United States. Those who had settled on land east of the Rio Grande River arranged to secede from Mexico and set up an independent country called the Republic of Texas. In 1845, Texas joined the United States. After the United States defeated Mexico in a war in 1848, Mexico had to give up what is now California, Nevada, Utah, Arizona, New Mexico and parts of Colorado, Kansas and Oklahoma.

In 1823, two years after it became independent, Mexico adopted a flag that reminds people of the Aztec past. At the center is a coat of arms showing an eagle perched on a cactus and holding a snake. The green stripe originally stood for independence, but today it symbolizes agriculture. The white, once the color of religious faith, now stands for peace. Red was for the union of the various Mexican states and is now for courage. Together, the stripes represent the United Mexican States, which is the official name of the country.

There are about 43,000,000 Mexicans, and Spanish is their official language. The majority are part Spanish and part Indian. Three million pure Indians speak only their own languages and follow their ancient tribal religions. Some also practice a mixture of Indian religion and Roman Catholicism. Catholicism has many followers in Mexico, but it is not now the official religion of the country, as it once was. Church and state are separate and the government owns the buildings where services are held. Priests and worshipers merely use churches and take care of them. *Member, United Nations.*

MONACO (MAHN-ah-ko): In the thirteenth century, members of a family called Grimaldi were forced to flee from political enemies in the Italian city of Genoa. Along the main road to the north, the refugees came upon a powerful fortress that took their fancy. Its name was Monaco, and whoever held it could control the trade route from Italy into France. One of the Grimaldis dressed up as a monk, stole into the fortress and, with the help of others in his party, captured it. Grimaldis have been in Monaco ever since. In 1512, the King of France declared that they had won the right to rule "from God and by the sword." In 1612, the leading member of the family assumed the title of Prince and, as head of an independent state, signed a treaty with France.

A member of the Grimaldi family still rules in the Principality of Monaco, which covers only 370 acres and has fewer than 25,000 inhabitants. Only one-third of the people who live there are native-born Monégasques, as they call themselves. The official language is French; the religion, Roman Catholic. The red and white Monégasque flag takes its colors from red and white diamonds (called *lozenges*) in the Grimaldi coat of arms.

MONGOLIA (mon-GO-lee-uh): The people of this very large country are descendants of the fierce Mongol soldiers who were once led by Genghis Khan. In the twelfth and thirteenth centuries they swept across Asia on their tough little ponies and conquered an empire that stretched from China to modern Czechoslovakia. Then one revolt after another forced the Mongols to retreat to their homeland. In the seventeenth century, they in turn became subjects of the Chinese and remained so for three hundred years.

After the Russian Revolution of 1917, some Mongolian soldiers and their leader Sukhebator rebelled against the Chinese. By 1921 they

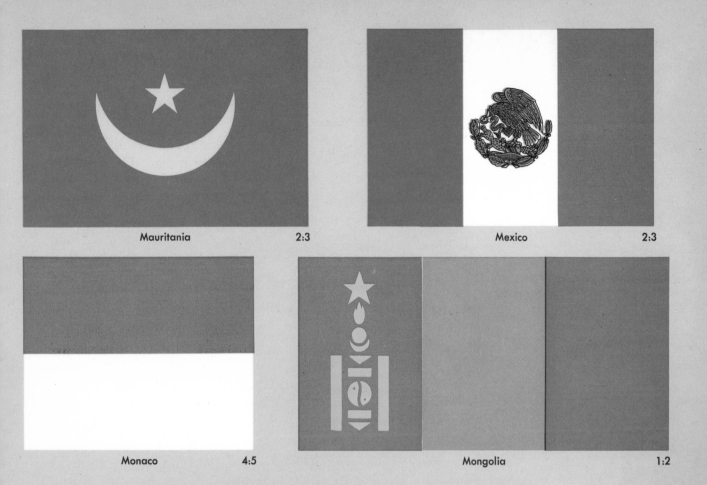

Mauritania 2:3

Mexico 2:3

Monaco 4:5

Mongolia 1:2

controlled the huge area which came to be called the Mongolian People's Republic or, sometimes, Outer Mongolia. Although the country was considered by most people to be part of China until 1945, it had its own pro-communist government and was under Soviet protection. It still remains an ally of the Soviet Union.

Sukhebator's revolutionary flag was a red banner with a gold *soyombo,* which, according to one interpretation, is a Mongolian symbol that stands for liberty and independence. It remains in the present flag, and along with the gold communist star, it tells a whole story without words. Beneath the star, a fire stands for life and continued prosperity. Next come the sun and moon, the mythical father and mother of the Mongols. Spearheads pointing downward signify "death to our enemies." Two horizontal rectangles, symbols of honesty and steadfastness, together mean that both the rulers and the ruled must be honest and serve well. Two fish symbolize men and women, wit, wisdom and vigilance. Therefore, the fishes say, "Let all men and women be wise guardians of their motherland." The vertical pillars stand for a Mongol proverb: "Two friends are stronger than stone walls." Thus all Mongols should be friends and so give strength to their land.

The *soyombo,* according to another interpretation, is an old religious design, and the fish are the Yin-Yang symbol (see KOREA).

The red of the flag not only stands for revolution, but is also an ancient Mongol symbol of love and victory. The blue, the traditional Mongol color, also stands for the sky which almost never has a cloud in it, and the gold of the *soyombo* represents unchanging friendship.

For all Mongolia's huge size, it has only about a million inhabitants, most of whom speak one of two Mongolian dialects. Although religion is not encouraged by the government, a number of Buddhist temples and monasteries still remain, and some people have ancient tribal religious beliefs.

Many Mongols live the life of herdsmen, very much as their ancestors did in the time of Genghis Khan. They keep horses, cattle, sheep, goats and camels, and travel with the herds from pasture to pasture. In the last forty years, more and more of these wandering groups have gathered in permanent settlements, and the number who can read and write has gone from almost none to about three-fourths of the population. *Member, United Nations.*

Father and son drinking tea, Morocco.

MOROCCO (moh-ROCK-oh): The Kingdom of Morocco, which became independent in 1956, was once part of the Arab empire that covered northwest Africa in the seventh century. At that time, Islam, the religion of Mohammed, was brought to Morocco, and most of the 14,000,000 Moroccans today are Moslems. There are also Roman Catholics whose ancestors became Christians after France and Spain began to control much of the old Arab empire.

Most Moroccans are descended from Arabs, but about 2,000,000 are Berbers whose ancestors were living in the country when the Arabs arrived. In the cities and towns near the coast there are a good many Jews, some of whose ancestors settled there more than two thousand years ago. Others arrived in the fifteenth century, when all Jews who would not join the Catholic Church were forced to leave Spain.

Spanish and French are taught in private schools; the Berbers speak a language of their own which has several dialects. The official language is Arabic, taught in a few religious schools. There is no compulsory education, and most Moroccans can neither read nor write.

The ancestors of the present king adopted an all-red flag in the seventeenth century. Then, in 1912, when France took control of the country, a five-pointed star was added to distinguish the Moroccan flag from others that were plain red. The same flag is still used today. *Member, United Nations.*

MUSCAT (MUS-cat) **AND OMAN** (oh-MAHN): The ruler of this small state, which runs in a narrow band along the southern and eastern tip of the Arabian Peninsula, is called a *sultan*. The country itself is the

Sultanate of Muscat and Oman and Dependencies, taking its name from the seaport city of Muscat and from one of its provinces, Oman.

On the stony hillsides of another province, Dhufar, grow large trees which once made its people wealthy. When the bark of the tree is cut, a bitter-tasting yellow liquid flows out and hardens into lumps of gum resin. These were gathered in ancient times and sent by caravan to Egypt, Palestine and other lands, where the gum was powdered to make sweet-smelling incense that was burned in temples. So great was the demand for this gum, which was called frankincense, that the growers could sell it for almost any price they asked. Then traders began to find other sources of supply, and they bypassed the old caravan route. Arabian coastlands no longer controlled the incense market, and for the last thousand years the people of Dhufar have lived in poverty.

Almost all of the country's 750,000 inhabitants are Arabs. The language is Arabic, and the official religion is Islam. A few Hindus, Roman Catholics and members of the Dutch Reformed Church live in the towns. The plain red flag is traditional all along the eastern Arabian coast, but it has special meaning here, because most of the people belong to an ancient Islamic group called Kharijites who first brought the red flag to the Persian Gulf.

A street scene in Nepal.

NEPAL (neh-PAHL): This ancient kingdom on the northeastern border of India has the world's highest peak, Mount Everest. And it has the only national flag in the world that is not a rectangle. Originally, the Nepalese carried two triangular pennants attached to the same staff. Perhaps a hundred years ago, the pennants were sewn together to make a flag of unusual shape, which is also a clue to Nepal's history.

The triangular shape and the red in the pennants are both traditional

101

among Hindus—and Nepal's ruling family and the majority of its people are, indeed, descended from Hindus who invaded the country from India in the eighteenth century. The invaders, known as Gurkhas, were famous warriors. Many of them still work as professional soldiers in the Indian and British armies.

The symbol in the flag's upper triangle is the moon, which represents the family of the king. The sun in the lower one stands for the Rana family who for many years had even more power than the king. The flag as a whole means: "May our country live as long as there is a sun and a moon." After an uprising in 1951, the Ranas lost most of their influence, but the traditional flag has not been changed.

About nine-tenths of Nepal's 9,400,000 people — those of Hindu ancestry — speak Nepali. The Newar, designers of the country's beautiful Buddhist temples, speak Newari. Sherpas, whose ancestors came from Tibet, are noted mountain climbers, and one of them accompanied an English mountaineer on the first successful climb to the top of Mount Everest in 1953. The Sherpas and various other groups have their own languages, but almost all speak Nepali, too. *Member, United Nations.*

NETHERLANDS: In 1568, William the Silent led the Dutch people in a revolt against the Spanish who ruled their country. William was a prince in a family called the House of Orange, which got its name in a roundabout way from a town in southern France. The town itself was called Orange, and because that also happened to be the name of a color, William's coat of arms included it, along with blue and white. The three colors of the House of Orange were used in the flag of the Netherlands after the revolt, and in 1599 the flag became official.

From the 1580's until 1813, the Netherlands was an independent republic, except for a few years when Napoleon held it as part of his empire. After 1650, a red stripe replaced the orange stripe in the flag. Historians do not agree on the reason for the change. Some say that the Dutch people thought red was a good republican color. Others believe that Dutch seamen complained because an orange stripe faded quickly in the salt sea air, and they asked for red, which they said lasted longer and was easier to see.

After the country (which was also called Holland) became the Kingdom of the Netherlands again, the old colors of the House of Orange were sometimes flown with the red, white and blue tricolor. However, the government, which is a constitutional monarchy, preferred the latter, and so it has become official.

The Netherlands is one of the most densely populated countries in the world. Its 12,300,000 people speak Dutch. Two out of five are Protestants, and an equal number Roman Catholics. The remainder follow various other religions or none at all. *Member, United Nations.*

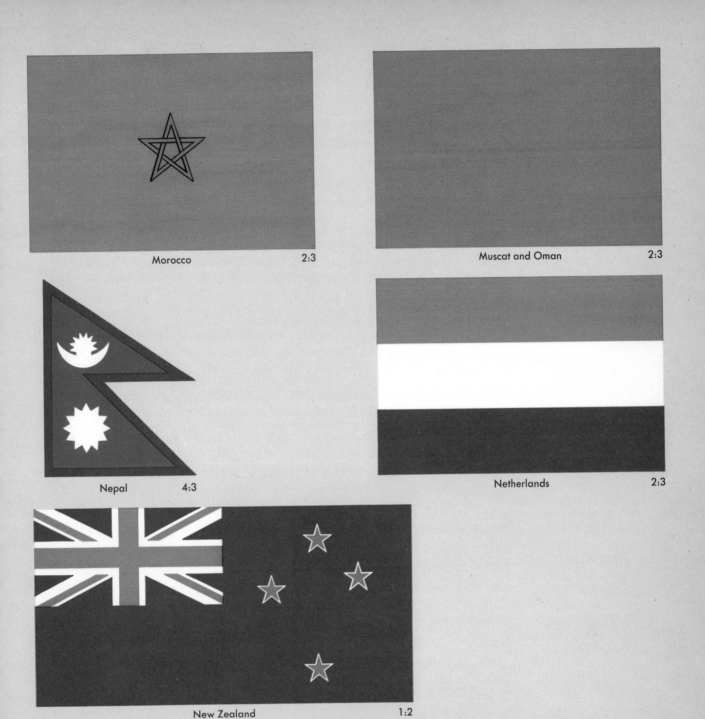

Morocco   2:3

Muscat and Oman   2:3

Nepal   4:3

Netherlands   2:3

New Zealand   1:2

NEW ZEALAND: Perhaps a thousand years ago, a boat carrying Polynesian men and women set out on a voyage to a small island in the South Pacific. They never reached their destination. Instead, they landed on one of two large islands that now make up New Zealand. Their descendants, the Maori (MAH-oh-ree) people, were living there when British immigrants arrived in the nineteenth century. By 1840, Britain had made New Zealand part of its colonial system.

In 1901, New Zealanders adopted a flag which had been used on

Maoris perform an ancient stick-game ceremony in New Zealand.

their ships for years and which closely resembled one chosen by Australia in the same year. It was blue with Britain's Union Flag in the canton, and it had stars that represented the constellation called the Southern Cross. Today that same flag is flown, although New Zealand ceased to be a British dominion in 1947 and became an independent member of the British Commonwealth of Nations.

Most of the 2,600,000 New Zealanders are of British origin and speak English. For the most part, they are Protestants — Presbyterian and Anglican — but with a good many Roman Catholics among them. Nearly 200,000 are Maoris, descendants of the original population. These dark-skinned citizens have the same rights as the light-skinned descendants of Europeans, and there are Maori members of Parliament. Many of them, however, cling to their own language and to some of their old tribal customs. *Member, United Nations.*

NICARAGUA (nick-uh-RAH-gwa): This was one of five countries that declared independence from Spain in 1821 and formed the Central American Federation. After the Federation ended in 1839, Nicaragua became a distinct, but not always free, nation. Its east coast was controlled by Britain for twenty years, and United States Marines occupied the country from 1912 to 1932.

The Republic of Nicaragua, along with two other countries (see EL SALVADOR), has kept the old blue and white flag of the Federation, but added its own emblem to the center stripe. The equilateral triangle in the emblem represents equality. (Some Nicaraguans say it also represents the three branches of the government.) A rainbow beneath the top point of the triangle symbolizes peace. A red Liberty Cap rises from five volcanoes which represent the five Central American republics and the desire of Nicaraguans for unity and brotherhood among them. The white in the flag stands for the purity of the nation, and the two blue stripes represent the Atlantic and Pacific Oceans.

More than three-fourths of the 1,700,000 Nicaraguans have both Indian and Spanish ancestry. The rest are pure European, pure Indian or pure Negro, or mixed Indian and Negro. The official language is Spanish. Many people also speak one of several Indian languages, and a few practice tribal religions. The majority are Roman Catholic. *Member, United Nations.*

NIGER (NYE-juhr): Part of Niger lies in the region where the kings of Songhai reigned from the fifteenth to the seventeenth century. Trade and gold brought tremendous wealth to Songhai. One of its rulers took with him several million dollars worth of gold pieces to give away when he made a pilgrimage to the holy Moslem city of Mecca. About 95 per cent of the people of Niger are still Moslems. (They call themselves Nigerois—a French word, pronounced nee-jair-wah—whereas those who live in Nigeria are Nigerians.) The Nigerois come from many tribes and speak many languages, only one of which has been written. French is the official government language, because France ruled the country from the nineteenth century until August 3, 1960, when it became the independent Republic of Niger.

Three-fourths of the 3,400,000 Nigerois have farms in the southern part of the country. The remainder belong to nomadic tribes that wander over the Sahara Desert in the north. Many of the nomads are Tuaregs who in former times were warriors and enemies of the old kingdom of Songhai. Now the Tuaregs make their living mostly by organizing caravans and raising livestock.

The flag of Niger was adopted in 1959, before independence. Its orange disc stands for the sun. The green stripe represents the fertile southern part of the country. The orange stripe is for the desert, and the white stands for purity. *Member, United Nations.*

A television studio in Niamey, Niger.

NIGERIA (nye-JEER-ee-uh): For thousands of years, people have been crowding into Nigeria, because it is a natural meeting-place of overland travel routes from the north and east. Now one-fifth of the people in the whole continent of Africa live in this country. They belong to 250 tribes, and each tribe has its own language. The largest is the Hausa, and its language is widely used as an intertribal tongue. Many Nigerians are Negroes. Others are related to Berbers and to Egyptians who came from far to the north and are not Negroes.

Most of the Hausa have been Moslems since the fourteenth century, but Islam is not the same among them as it is in the Arab world.

Negroes, not Arabs, brought Islam to Nigeria, and in this country a form of religion developed that comes partly from the Koran (the sacred book of the Moslems) and partly from old tribal beliefs. Nearly half of all the 57,000,000 Nigerians call themselves Moslems. Most of them live in the north and west. In the south and east live Christians, many of them members of the Ibo tribe. Christians make up less than a quarter of the population. Nearly a third of the Nigerians have been very little influenced by either Islam or Christianity.

In the nineteenth century, when powerful countries in Europe were seizing parts of Africa, a British trading company took control of the area of Nigeria, which had never been united before. In 1914, it was made a British colony. On October 1, 1960, it became the independent Federal Republic of Nigeria. As independence drew near in 1959, there was a national contest for a flag design. The winner, among 2,870 Nigerians who entered, was a young engineer. In his flag the green stands for fertile agricultural land, the white for peace and unity.

Both peace and unity have been hard for Nigeria to achieve. On May 30, 1967, the Eastern Region, where Ibos are the majority, seceded and established the independent Republic of Biafra. Because the outcome of the war between Nigeria and Biafra was uncertain late in 1968, the Biafran flag is not shown. *Member, United Nations.*

A chemistry class in a women's college, Nigeria.

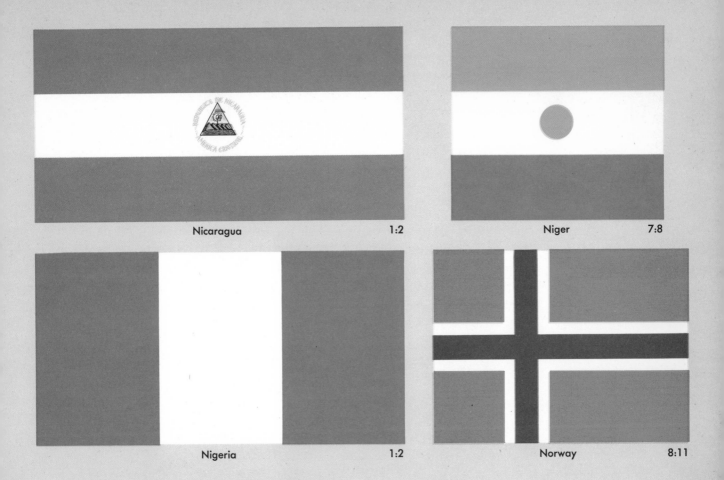

Nicaragua 1:2

Niger 7:8

Nigeria 1:2

Norway 8:11

NORWAY (NOR-way) is a beautiful country of lakes and mountains and fjords (long bays reaching inland from the sea), but it has very little good farmland. And so, in the ninth century, Norwegian sailors began adventuring away from home in their sturdy boats. Because they came from fjord country, they were called vikings, which means "people of the bays."

At that time many seacoast towns of Europe were rich in goods and treasure, and the vikings claimed a share of it. Some of it they got by peaceful trade, some by raiding and plundering. Expeditions took many of them far from Norway, even into the western Mediterranean Sea and across the North Atlantic to Greenland, then to America. Others conquered part of France and settled there—in a region still called Normandy because it was ruled by Norsemen (another name for vikings).

The great viking expansion lasted for more than two hundred years. In modern times there was another great movement away from Norway with its too-little farmland. Hundreds of thousands of Norwegians went to other countries, especially the United States.

The 3,800,000 people who live in Norway today speak Norwegian, which has two forms. Both are official, and children study both in school. One form is the ancient traditional tongue that was much influenced by Danish. The other is a modern language that has grown out of local dialects spoken by the common people. About 20,000 Lapps in northern Norway speak Finnish (see SWEDEN).

From 1380 to 1814, Norway was part of Denmark and had no flag of its own. Then for almost a hundred years Norway and Sweden were united. During this period, Norway adopted its own flag which sometimes flew over both countries. At other times, the Swedish flag was used by both. Since 1898, Norway has used its own flag. In 1905, it separated from Sweden, becoming an independent constitutional monarchy with its own king. The cross in its flag reflects the Christian tradition which began in Norway about the time the viking period ended. Norway has an official religion—Evangelical Lutheran—but all religions are permitted. *Member, United Nations.*

Village schoolboys studying, Pakistan.

PAKISTAN (PACK-i-stan): When India won its freedom from Britain in 1947, two distinct new countries were formed. One was India; the other was the Islamic Republic of Pakistan, which has two widely separated parts. At their closest points, West Pakistan and East Pakistan are about nine hundred miles apart.

108

The founder of the new country, Mohammed Ali Jinnah, designed a flag based on one that had been used for forty years as a symbol of an organization called the Moslem League. The white in this flag represented the minority communities of Pakistan, consisting of Hindus, Christians, Parsees and others. The green represented Islam, as did the crescent and star. More than 85 per cent of the 103,000,000 Pakistanis are Moslem.

In 1964, Pakistan gave a new symbolic meaning to the flag. The white now represents peace. Green is for prosperity. The crescent stands for progress, and the star represents light and knowledge.

Most people in East Pakistan speak Bengali. Those in West Pakistan speak a great variety of languages, but almost everyone understands Urdu, a language brought to the area by the Hindu servants of Mongol conquerors in the twelfth and thirteenth centuries. Both Urdu and Bengali are used in the schools, but less than one-fifth of the people can read or write any language at all. English is used by the government and in colleges and universities. *Member, United Nations.*

PANAMA (PAN-uh-ma): The Isthmus of Panama, which is in the southernmost part of Central America, was once part of Colombia. Some of the people in this narrow strip of land wanted to separate from Colombia, and in 1903, their leader, Dr. Manuel Amador Guerrero, went to Washington, D.C. to ask help for the secession movement. At that same time, the United States government was trying to get from Colombia the right to build a canal across Panama. While discussions went on, United States warships near the coast of Panama had orders to keep any armed forces from landing there. (This was a way of making sure that Colombia could not send troops to prevent the secession of Panama.)

In October, the Colombian government decided against the canal, and Dr. Amador went home to prepare a breakaway from Colombia. Among other things, he asked his son, who was an artist, to design a flag. Dr. Amador's wife then sewed the flag according to her son's instructions and finished it on November 2. The next day, Panama declared independence. Dr. Amador raised the new flag and two weeks later the new government granted the United States the right to rule forever in the part of the country through which the canal was to pass.

Panama still uses its first flag. Young Amador, who designed it, said he did not intend it to have any special meaning. But Panamanians now say this is what their flag stands for: the blue section represents the Conservative Party; the red is for the Liberal Party, the white for peace and unity between these rival parties in the cause of independence. The blue star represents purity and honesty in the government and the red star symbolizes law and authority. About 1,200,000 people live in the Republic of Panama. Two-thirds of them are part Indian and part Spanish. The other third are in about equal proportions Indian, Negro and descendants of Europeans. The Indians belong to three tribal groupings that have different languages and customs. Spanish is the official language, and most Panamanians are Roman Catholics. *Member, United Nations.*

A broom-seller on her way to market, Paraguay.

PARAGUAY (PAIR-uh-gwigh): This is the only country in the world that has different emblems on the front and back of its national flag. On one side appears the national coat of arms—a five pointed star surrounded by palm and olive branches tied at the bottom with a red, white and blue ribbon. On the reverse side is an emblem called the Treasury Seal which bears the Spanish words for Peace and Justice, together with a lion and a red Liberty Cap representing freedom (see page 38).

The emblems were added to the flag in 1842, but the colors date from the year after the country won independence in 1811, earlier than Spain's other South American colonies. Unlike many other countries, it achieved freedom and became a republic almost without bloodshed. However, its president later allowed the country to get involved in a war with Argentina, Uruguay and Brazil, all three at once, and in the fighting which went on from 1865 to 1870, almost 80 per cent of the Paraguayan people were killed. Out of 1,200,000 Paraguayans at the beginning of the war, only about 200,000 women and 28,000 men were still alive at the end.

In the hundred years since then, the population has grown to more than 2,000,000, largely a mixture of Europeans and Guaraní Indians. Most people speak both Spanish and a form of Guaraní, which has borrowed many Spanish words. The president, according to law, must be a Roman Catholic, and the Roman Catholic Church is the state church, with everyone paying taxes to support it. *Member, United Nations.*

PERU (peh-ROO): Indians have been in Peru for about ten thousand years. At first they lived very simply; then gradually they developed more and more skills, until, by the eleventh century, people began to live in cities where potters, jewelers and weavers of textiles were supported by a well organized system of farming. Later, when the Inca Indians ruled over a huge empire, they engineered a network of roads, built palaces and temples of stone and accumulated great wealth. In 1532, Spanish invaders destroyed the Inca civilization and began nearly three centuries of colonial rule.

In 1820, when much of South America was in rebellion, a revolutionary hero, José de San Martín, landed in Peru to help liberate the country from Spain. As he stepped ashore, he saw a flock of beautiful white and red birds rise up, flying free, from the shore. Later, when he

110

Pakistan   2:3

Panama   2:3

Paraguay (obverse)   1:2

Peru   2:3

designed a flag for the new Republic of Peru, which became independent in 1821, San Martín remembered the birds which seemed to him to have the spirit of liberty. So the white of their breasts became the white of the flag, and the red stood for their wings.

On the state flag, the coat of arms, designed later, suggested the country's natural wealth: the llama, a kind of camel which is a useful burden-bearer, stood for the animal world; a cinchona tree, from which the drug quinine is made, represented the plant world; and a cornucopia overflowing with gold coins symbolized Peru's minerals. The coat of arms does not appear on the national flag.

Nearly half of the 11,700,000 Peruvians are descendants of the Quechua Indians, who built the Inca civilization, or of the Aymarás who lived there before Inca times. Ten per cent of the people are pure Spanish. Others are part Indian and part Spanish. A smaller group is descended from Negro slaves brought to Peru by the Spaniards, and along the coast are a few Chinese and Japanese. The official language of Peru is Spanish. All children who attend school must use it, although the mother tongue of a great many Peruvians is Quechua or Aymará. Other Indian languages are also spoken by small groups. Many Indians keep all or part of their traditional tribal religions, but officially the whole country is Roman Catholic. *Member, United Nations.*

111

PHILIPPINES (FILL-uh-peens): The first European visit to the Philippine Islands was made in 1521 by the Portuguese explorer Ferdinand Magellan. Spanish explorers came later, and gradually the Philippines became a Spanish colony.

In the 1890's, Filipinos organized a revolution against their Spanish rulers and adopted various flags, most of which had a triangle as a symbol. The leader of the revolution, General Emilio Aguinaldo, designed the one that was raised when the Philippines declared their independence from Spain in 1898. This flag did not fly for long, because the United States invaded the Philippines, fought against the revolutionaries, and began to rule the country. In 1935, the islands won an agreement promising them independence in ten years, and the old revolutionary flag was chosen to fly alongside the flag of the United States.

During World War II, the Japanese occupied the Philippines for three years. After the war, in 1946, the country became independent, and once more began to fly the flag that Aguinaldo had designed nearly fifty years before. The old general was still living at the time.

The white triangle in the flag stands for the revolution of the 1890's. The eight rays of the sun stand for the first eight provinces that rebelled against Spain. Three stars represent the three main groups of the islands. Red stands for courage, blue for high political ideals, white for purity and peace. In time of peace, the blue stripe is flown at the top. In time of war, the red is on top.

The official national language of the Philippine Republic is Tagalog (tah-GAH-log), one of 84 used by the country's 33,000,000 people. Only 45 per cent of all Filipinos speak it. Almost as many can speak English and Spanish, which are also official. About four-fifths of the people are Roman Catholic. The others are Protestant, Moslem, Buddhist or members of the Philippine Independent Church. *Member, United Nations.*

A tobacco farmer in the Philippines.

POLAND: A white eagle on a red background was the coat of arms of a Polish prince in the Middle Ages. In 1241, this design became the coat of arms of the Polish state. In the fifteenth and sixteenth centuries, Poland grew to be a very powerful country that ruled over lands far beyond its present borders—east into Russia and south into Hungary. But by the late eighteenth century, Poland had completely lost its independence and was apportioned among other countries. After Austria and Germany were defeated in World War I, Poland regained independence, and in 1918 it adopted a flag with two broad horizontal stripes, the upper one white and the lower, red. These colors had come from the old Polish coat of arms.

During World War II, Poland was conquered by armies from Nazi Germany. Then it became independent again at the end of the war, this time with a communist government, and it took a new name, the Polish

Polish children learn arithmetic with the help of an abacus.

People's Republic, but made no change in the flag that had been adopted in 1918. Also, the coat of arms, which had first been made official in 1241, remained the same, except that after 1944 there was no crown on the eagle's head.

The 31,700,000 Poles belong to a family of peoples called Slavs. Their ancestors, who seem to have been one of the early tribes in Europe, pushed out eastward and southward and settled in what are now parts of Russia, Byelorussia, the Ukraine, Czechoslovakia, Bulgaria and Yugoslavia. The Polish language is related to Russian, but is written in the Latin alphabet instead of the Russian Cyrillic alphabet. All education in Poland is free.

According to one estimate, 96 per cent of the Poles regularly attend Roman Catholic church services, although the Communist Party, which controls the government, has had strong disagreements with the leaders of the church. *Member, United Nations.*

PORTUGAL (POR-choo-gul) became an independent country in the twelfth century when the Moslems, who had been its rulers, were driven out and a Christian monarchy established. In the fifteenth century, daring Portuguese explorers, who had mastered the art of navigation, visited lands unknown to other Europeans. A Portuguese ship was the first to sail all the way around the earth. By the middle of the sixteenth

113

Oxen, with typical harness, hitched to plow, Portugal.

century, the Portuguese king ruled over a vast empire with territories in South America, Africa, India, China and elsewhere.

The monarchy and some of the empire lasted until the revolution in 1910 which established the Republic of Portugal. In 1932, Prime Minister Antonio de Oliveira Salazar took office. He headed the government until September, 1968, exercising dictatorial powers.

Portugal still has colonies, including Mozambique, Angola and Portuguese Guinea in Africa, and Macao near Canton in China. In Portugal itself there are 9,200,000 people whose language is Portuguese and whose religion is Roman Catholic. Among the 13,000,000 in the colonies are people from many African tribes who have their own tribal language and religion.

The flag, adopted after the 1910 revolution, is rich green and scarlet. The green stands for hope, the scarlet for blood shed for freedom. The coat of arms, inherited from the monarchy, is very old. Its many symbols include five shields in the form of a cross which calls attention to a victory over five Moslem princes. There is also an armillary sphere, a device used by astronomers in the fifteenth century when Portuguese navigators were ahead of all others in exploring the world. *Member, United Nations.*

QATAR (KAH-tar or GAH-tar) is a small peninsula extending like a thumb from Arabia into the Persian Gulf. The head of its government, called The Ruler, is a sheik, or Arab chieftain. Most of its 60,000 people are Arabs and Moslems, and they speak Arabic. Children also learn English in the growing number of public schools made possible by the discovery of oil. According to an agreement signed in 1916, the foreign affairs of Qatar are conducted by Great Britain. In all other matters, decisions are made by The Ruler with the help of a Deputy-Ruler and an Advisory Council.

The Qatari flag goes back to the time when all ships of the northeastern coast of Arabia had red flags. About a hundred years ago, the Qataris added a white area near the hoist to set it off from the flags of their neighbors. The white strip is wider than a similar strip on the flag of Bahrain. Until recently the Qataris colored the cloth with a special dye which, although bright red at first, turned a deep maroon after being exposed to the sun for a while. In 1949, they decided to adopt the darker color officially. It has become known as Qatar maroon.

114

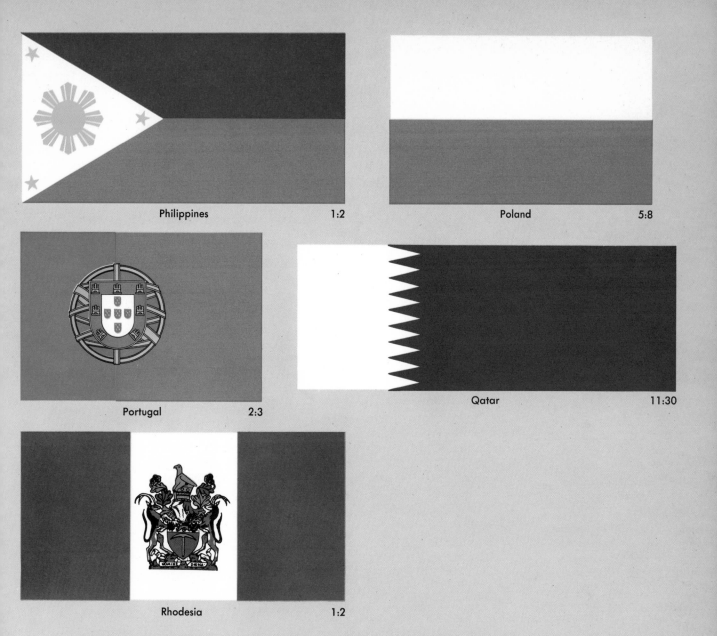

Philippines   1:2

Poland   5:8

Portugal   2:3

Qatar   11:30

Rhodesia   1:2

RHODESIA (ro-DEE-zhya): In 1965, the 220,000 Europeans in this African country declared their independence from Britain. At that time, Britain had been insisting that equal rights must be given to the 4,300,-000 African Rhodesians. Rather than grant equality, the white Rhodesians broke their former ties with Britain. On November 11, 1968, they adopted a new flag, but kept the coat of arms given to the country when it was a British colony called Southern Rhodesia.

The flag's green stripes stand for agriculture. In the arms, the carving of a bird found at the Great Zimbabwe Ruins symbolizes the past. The golden pick represents mining. The red lion and thistles come from the family arms of Cecil Rhodes, an Englishman who founded the country, and the Latin motto, translated, means "May she be worthy of the name." Cecil Rhodes, in the 1800's, saw the vast wealth in that part of the world. He and many other powerful men believed that a strong country had a right to take over weaker ones if it could, so he helped his government annex southern Africa to the British Empire. Once, when he was explaining his ambitions, he said, "I would annex the planets, if I could!"

The majority of Rhodesians practice their own tribal religions and speak one of several African languages. Many people also know either Swahili or English, or both. English is the official language of the Christian European minority. A group of men who have gone into exile in Zambia have formed the Zimbabwe African People's Union, which plans to take over the government when it can. Zimbabwe is the name of an impressive ruined city in Rhodesia which has become a symbol of great things that Africans achieved in the days before Europeans arrived.

Romania: country people in traditional costumes.

ROMANIA (roh-MAIN-yuh): After Roman armies conquered this part of Europe at the beginning of the second century, many settlers moved in, and soon everyone there was speaking a dialect of Latin. This developed into the language that is used by most of the 19,500,000 Romanians today. It is called a Romance language because it comes from the tongue of ancient Rome. (Other Romance languages are Italian, Spanish, Catalan, Portuguese, French and Romansh, spoken in Switzerland.)

116

Because their country is sandwiched between Slavic nations—Bulgaria, Yugoslavia and the Ukraine—the Romanians have adopted many Slavic words. They have also borrowed from neighboring Hungarians, from Greeks who were once busy traders along their coast on the Black Sea, and from Turks who ruled the country for centuries.

Under the Turks, Romania consisted of two provinces. In 1848, some people from both provinces tried to unite and win independence, and at that time they adopted a flag with horizontal stripes—blue, yellow and red. The rebellion failed, but in 1859 the two provinces did achieve union and partial independence. Two years later, the united country adopted the name Romania because of its ancient connection with Rome. In 1866, when a German prince became king of Romania, he changed the stripes in the flag from horizontal to vertical.

After World War II, a communist-controlled government was established in Romania, and in 1948 the king had to leave. At that time a national emblem was added to the flag, showing mountains and forests surrounded by sheaves of wheat to represent natural resources. The communist five-pointed red star was added to the emblem in 1952. In 1965, the name *Republica Socialista România* was also added.

The predominant religion in Romania is Eastern Orthodox. There are also members of other Christian denominations, as well as Jews and Moslems. *Member, United Nations.*

RWANDA (ruh-WAHN-dah): For a long time, farmers who belonged to the Hutu tribe were the main inhabitants of this beautiful mountain country in Africa. Alongside the farmers lived a small group of hunters called Twa who are relatives of the Pygmies. Then, three or four hundred years ago, a tribe of very tall people called Tutsi (or Batusi or Watusi) invaded the country from the direction of Ethiopia. The Tutsi had herds of big-horned cattle and were fierce warriors. Although the

Girl of the Hutu tribe, Rwanda.

Hutu outnumbered them ten to one, the Hutu and Twa were very soon ruled by the Tutsi.

The Hutu had to take care of the conquerors' cattle. A man who owned many cattle had a great deal of influence, and cattle are still important. Many Rwandans will not eat vegetables and drink milk at the same meal. They believe that if they do they may bring harm to the cows that give the milk.

In 1885 and 1886, when the big countries of Europe divided most of Africa into colonies, Germany got Rwanda. After Germany was defeated in World War I, the victorious nations gave Rwanda to Belgium, which kept the Tutsi king in power. In 1959, the Hutu majority began to revolt against both the Tutsi and the Belgians. At the end of this civil war, the Hutu won a nationwide election and, on July 1, 1962, declared the independence of the Republic of Rwanda.

The red stripe in the country's flag stands for the bloodshed and suffering endured to achieve freedom. Yellow is for victory of the revolution. Green is for hope, and *R* is for Rwanda.

Most of the 3,000,000 Rwandans speak the language called Kinyarwanda, which, along with French, is official. More than half of the people practice the religions of their own tribes. About one-third are Roman Catholics and a few are Protestants. *Member, United Nations.*

SAN MARINO (san muh-REE-no): The twenty-three square miles of this small republic are in high mountains entirely surrounded by Italy. Only one road leads up to the town, also called San Marino, where most of the 17,000 citizens live. An ancient wall with forts encloses the town, but there is no real army. The 180 soldiers in the country merely take part in ceremonies.

In the center of the town stands a hermitage that is supposed to have been built in A.D. 441. According to tradition, the country itself has existed longer than the hermitage. It probably has. The Samarrenese people say that theirs is the oldest republic in the world and the oldest state of any kind in Europe. Although there have been several flags, the present one was adopted about 1797. Its stripes stand for the whiteness of the snowy peaks and for the blue of the sky and the Adriatic Sea not far away. The coat of arms shows stone towers on the three mountain tops in the country, and under them is the Latin word for liberty.

The Republic of San Marino is governed by a Council of sixty members chosen in an election in which both men and women vote. Every six months the Council selects two of its members to act as executive officers. So careful has the government been that the country has no debt, although a complete social security plan covers all citizens from birth to death. The official language of the country is Italian. Its people are Roman Catholic.

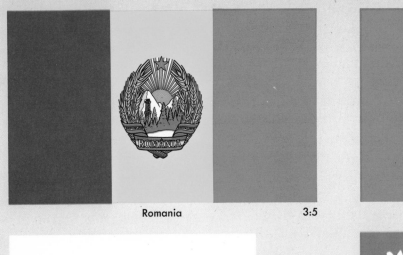

Romania   3:5

Rwanda   2:3

San Marino   3:4

Saudi Arabia   2:3

SAUDI ARABIA (sah-oo-dee ah-RAY-bee-uh): Mohammed, founder of the religion called Islam, was born in Arabia some time between A.D. 570 and 580. In the seventh century, militant believers in Mohammed's faith set out from Arabia to spread the new religion. Before long they had conquered and converted all of North Africa, then moved to Spain.

Islam also spread eastward as far as Central Asia and reached the Malay Peninsula and Indonesia. In many places where Arab armies or traders or missionaries went, the people adopted the Arabic language, and they still speak it. Today nearly half a billion people follow the religion that began in Arabia. Only one other religion in the world has more followers—Christianity.

After years of Arab expansion, the desert country of Arabia lost its influence while other parts of the Moslem world grew more important. For a long time Arabia was not even independent. Turkey ruled over it until in 1916 it broke away. The first king of the new Arabia chose a flag that had long been used by independent tribes in the area. It was green, supposedly the favorite color of Mohammed—and to desert people the color of paradise. A white sword stood for the struggle to carry Islam far and wide. The sword and the Arabic words above it were sewn on both sides of the flag, so that no matter which side an Arab

119

looked at he could read their message: "There is no God but Allah, and Mohammed is the Prophet of Allah."

The flag remains the same, but the country is now called the Kingdom of Saudi Arabia because the king comes from a family named Saud. The discovery of oil has given enormous wealth to the king, who is an absolute ruler. For years the royal family passed along very little of their income to the 7,500,000 Arabs, many of whom are nomads living just as their ancestors have lived for hundreds of years. But education is now beginning—there are three hundred schools in the country. An enormous new plant for de-salting sea water will make more farming possible, and several new industries are growing. *Member, United Nations.*

SENEGAL (sen-eh-GAHL): A state called Tekrur grew up along the Senegal River in West Africa in the eleventh or twelfth century. Four hundred years later, another state called Futa took its place, but when European slave-hunters invaded West Africa, Futa disappeared. To protect the slave traders, the Portuguese built forts on the Senegal River. Then the Dutch captured the forts, and later the French seized control. After that, the French and British were rivals for a long time. Finally the contest ended in the nineteenth century with the British holding a narrow strip of land on each side of the Gambia River and the French ruling the territory all around it and northward to the Senegal River.

In the French area, on the very westernmost tip of Africa, a port called Dakar had long served as a collection place for slaves, with special buildings that could hold five thousand at a time. Dakar was important because it lay closer to the Americas than any other point in Africa. It is still important for the same reason. Planes use its big international airport, and a dozen ships a day enter or leave the harbor. Outgoing vessels are likely to carry cargoes of peanuts, the biggest crop in the modern land of Senegal.

In 1959 Senegal joined in an independent federation with the country now called Mali. The two countries separated in 1960, and the Republic of Senegal continued to use the colors of the federation flag, but added a five-pointed green star which stands for mankind.

The 3,500,000 Senegalese belong to several tribes, and many members of each tribe keep their traditional religion. Some have also been converted to Roman Catholicism, the faith of many of the 40,000 Europeans in Senegal. Two African languages, Wolof and Fula, are widely spoken, and the educated Senegalese speak French, the official language of the government. *Member, United Nations.*

SIERRA LEONE (see-AIR-uh lee-OWN): About 2,300,000 people live in this former British colony on the west coast of Africa. English is the official language. Tribal groups speak thirteen different languages, two of which have written forms.

The name of the country, meaning "Mountain Range of the Lion," originated among Portuguese sailors, who said the mountain peaks along its coast always seemed to be surrounded by roaring thunderstorms. Freetown, the capital city, established in 1787 as a home for freed slaves, now has a population of 50,000, a great many of whom are descendants of the original settlers.

Sierra Leone became independent on April 27, 1961, and its flag, which had been selected in a competition, was raised for the first time. Green represents the vegetation of this agricultural country, white stands for peace, and blue for the nearby ocean.

About one-third of the Sierra Leoneans are Moslems, a slightly smaller number have been converted to Christianity, and most of the others practice the religions of their tribes. In several tribes there are secret societies which have a number of duties: they settle disputes and supervise trading; they treat various sicknesses; they conduct religious ceremonies and educate children in the ways of their people. For young men and women who are being trained in modern schools, these societies are still important, but much less so than in the past. *Member, United Nations.*

SIKKIM (SICK-im): This tiny state in the Himalaya Mountains is surrounded by India, China, Bhutan and Nepal. Its 180,000 people, mostly farmers, raise food for their own country and two main crops for export—orchids and a spice called cardamon. Nepalese make up about two thirds of the population; about one-fifth are Lepchas who may have been the original inhabitants. There are also some Bhotias whose ancestors came from the neighboring Tibetan part of China. The most widely used language is Nepali; Lepchas and Bhotias speak Sikkimese.

Although a good many of the people are Hindu, Buddhism is the official religion, and the symbol at the center of the Sikkimese flag is the Buddhist Wheel of the Law. Such a wheel stands for orderly change and progress. At its center is the Yin-Yang symbol (see KOREA, MONGOLIA). The red border around the flag stands for the high mountains that surround this small monarchy.

India, which manages Sikkim's foreign affairs, defense and finances, also appoints the Prime Minister. The ruler is a king, or *chogyal,* sometimes also called *maharajah* in Hindi. In 1963, the king married a young woman from the United States whose title is *gyalmo,* or queen.

Man and wife selling jewelry, Sikkim.

SINGAPORE (SING-ah-pohr): Just off the tip of the Malay Peninsula lies a large island that once had powerful rulers who called their main seaport Singhapura, meaning "City of the Lion." About six hundred years ago the country was defeated in a struggle with neighboring people, and by the nineteenth century almost no one lived there. In 1819, the island and the city, both called Singapore by the British, became part of Britain's colonial system and remained so until after World War II. For a while Singapore was one of the fourteen states in the new country of Malaysia. Then, on August 9, 1965, it withdrew and became an independent parliamentary republic.

The flag adopted in 1959 for Singapore's 2,000,000 people is red and white, like many flags in Southeast Asia. The red stripe stands for universal brotherhood and the equality of man. The white means everlasting purity and virtue. The new moon suggests by its shape that the country is a new one, just beginning. The five stars stand for democracy, peace, progress, justice and equality.

Originally, the people of the island were Malays, and the Malay tongue remains the national language. However, two-thirds are now of Chinese origin, and Chinese is also an official language. The Tamil language, spoken by many Indians, and English, which is used in government work, are official, too.

Singapore: Chinese longshoremen unloading a ship.

All religions are permitted. The six largest are Islam, Christianity, Buddhism, Hinduism, Confucianism, Taoism. *Member, United Nations.*

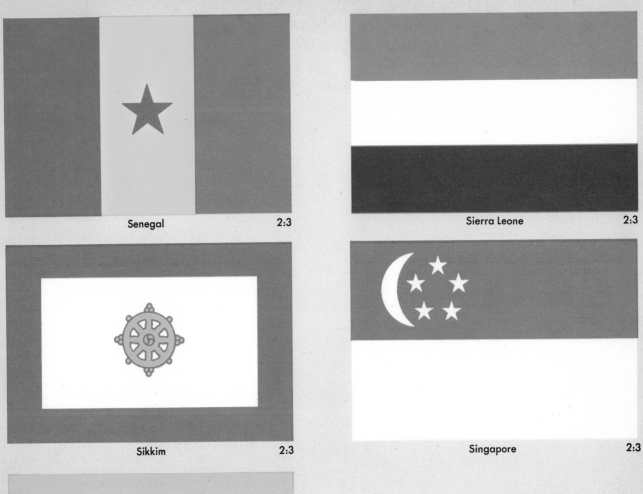

Senegal   2:3

Sierra Leone   2:3

Sikkim   2:3

Singapore   2:3

Somalia   2:3

SOMALIA (soh-MAHL-yuh): Nearly 2,500,000 people, many of whom
are wandering herders of camels and sheep, live in the two provinces of
the Somali Republic which were formerly colonies held by Britain and
Italy. An equal number of Somalis occupy three other areas—one in
Ethiopia, one in Kenya and one in French Somaliland. This division of
their ancient pasture lands was made more by Europeans than by Africans, and the flag of the Somalis reflects how they feel about the problem. Its star has five points—two for the united provinces and three for
the areas where Somalis are still under foreign rule. The blue and white

123

of the flag, designed in 1954, symbolizes the United Nations which supervised the country after World War II until it achieved independence in 1960. According to its constitution, the country is bound to use peaceful means in trying to unite all five areas.

Almost everyone in Somalia speaks the Somali language, but it has not yet been written down. The official languages in which the government does business are English, Italian and Arabic. Arabic is taught in the schools. The constitution specifies that the president must be a Moslem. *Member, United Nations.*

SOUTH AFRICA: The flag of South Africa tells much about its history. The large orange, white and blue stripes come from the early seventeenth-century Dutch flag (see NETHERLANDS). They remind South Africans that the first permanent European settlers came there from the Netherlands. After the Dutch landed in 1652, they began to rule the olive-skinned Hottentots who lived near the Cape of Good Hope. Soon the Dutch were learning some words from the Hottentots and other words from French settlers. Gradually the language they spoke took on a new sound, and in time it became a distinct new language—Afrikaans. Today more than half the whites in South Africa speak Afrikaans and are known as Afrikaaners or Boers (BOORZ), a Dutch word for farmers.

In 1806 Britain took over the area, called it Cape Colony, and for many years after that ruled both the white Boers and the black Africans who had moved in from the north. The British Union Flag in the white stripe of the South African flag stands for this stage in its history.

Many Boers did not like British rule. They objected because the British made it first hard, then impossible for them to keep slaves. To escape from regulation, many thousands of Boers went on the Great Trek, or migration, northward in covered wagons and founded two new republics, the Transvaal and the Orange Free State. These republics had their own flags until 1902, when they lost the Boer War and were added by the British to Cape Colony. In 1927, their flags were placed alongside the British Union Flag in the white stripe of the old Dutch flag to form the flag of South Africa.

The flags of the two conquered republics had their own stories. The one flown by the Orange Free State had been given to the Free Staters by the King of the Netherlands and was designed to remind them of their Dutch origin. In its canton was a modern Dutch flag, and it had orange stripes because that was a traditional color in the king's family, which was known as the House of Orange. The flag of Transvaal also was a modern Dutch flag to which a perpendicular green stripe had been added at the hoist.

In 1910, the British colony of Natal joined Cape Colony to form the Union of South Africa which, in 1931, became a member of the British Commonwealth of Nations. South Africa continued to fly the complex 1927 flag, even after it withdrew from the Commonwealth in 1961 and changed its name to the Republic of South Africa. The reason for withdrawal was that other Commonwealth nations objected strongly to the South African government's policy of *apartheid* (pronounced ah-PART-hate).

Apartheid means apartness or separation of the 18,000,000 people, according to their physical types. Black Africans, who make up two-thirds of the population but who cannot be elected to parliament, must live in special settlements and carry passes whenever they go outside these areas. White South Africans, who call themselves Europeans, are about one-sixth of the population and have control of parliament and the government. Others who come under certain provisions of the apartheid laws are Asians, mostly from India, and people called Cape Coloureds, who are part Dutch and part Hottentot.

Most of the Africans speak their own languages; many of the Asians speak Hindi. The Cape Coloureds and the Europeans speak English and Afrikaans, the official languages. Most Europeans and Cape Coloureds belong to the Dutch Reformed Church or the Church of England. Most Africans are Christians, but about 4,000,000 follow tribal religions. Asians are Hindu, Moslem or Jain. *Member, United Nations.*

SPAIN: Early in the eighth century, Moslem invaders began to cross from Africa into Spain and conquered almost the whole country. Then gradually the Christians forced the Moslems to leave, and by 1492 the last of them had been defeated. As Moslem power dwindled, small Christian kingdoms grew. Two of them—Aragon and Castile—united in 1479, and after that the joint monarchy finally brought all Spain under its rule.

While the kingdoms were still separate, four of them had red in their colors and two also had gold. In 1785, King Charles III officially adopted a red and gold flag. In 1931, when a revolution overthrew the monarchy and established a republic, the flag was changed. Five years later a group of Spanish generals, aided by Nazi Germany and Fascist Italy, began a war of rebellion against the Republic, and in 1936 they revived the old red and gold flag. On it they placed a coat of arms in which an eagle holds a shield bearing the symbol of several old Spanish kingdoms, plus the Pillars of Hercules, which represent the land on either side of the Straits of Gibraltar. When the rebellion finally succeeded, this became the state flag of the new government, which declared its opposition to democracy and called the country the Spanish

State. The head of government was General Francisco Franco, whose title was Leader. (The coat of arms does not appear on the national flag.)

About 31,600,000 people live in Spain, and Spanish is the official language, spoken by two-thirds of the people. The other third speak either Galician, which is similar to Portuguese, or Catalan, which is similar to French, or Basque. The latter does not resemble any other language in the world and it is so hard, say the Basque people, that "even the devil can't learn it."

Roman Catholicism is the religion of the people and of the state. All government officials must be members of the Church, and the Catholic faith must be taught in all schools. The government appoints all high church officers and pays the salaries of all clergymen. *Member, United Nations.*

SUDAN (soo-DAN): About 2,700 years ago, people called Nubians lived along the Nile River, south of Egypt, in what is now Sudan. From time to time the Egyptians attacked them, but finally a powerful Nubian army fell upon their enemy, conquered them and ruled Egypt for nearly a hundred years until other invaders drove them out. The Nubians were skillful iron makers. Today they still use the same ingenious smelting methods their ancestors invented long ago.

A local government official in the Sudan.

When Arabs began to move southward on the continent of Africa, they were surprised to find that not only the Nubians, but also the other people south of the Sahara Desert had dark skins. They began to call the whole continent, from the Indian Ocean west to the Atlantic Ocean, Bilad-as-Sudan, meaning "Land of the Black People." In 1822, Egypt conquered the eastern part of the Sudan and governed it until 1870. Then British generals ruled until they were driven out by Moslem armies.

In 1896, British and Egyptian forces joined to regain control of the Sudan, and from 1899 till 1951 their flags flew side by side on all government buildings in what was called the Anglo-Egyptian Sudan.

On January 1, 1956, the flag of the newly independent Republic of the Sudan flew for the first time. Its colors stand for the kind of country in which the Sudanese live: blue is for the Nile River, yellow is for the irrigated sands of the desert, and green is for the crops.

There are more than a dozen tribal groups among the 14,000,000 Sudanese, each with its own language and religion. Those in the north, including the Nubians, are mostly Moslems. The official language of the country and its schools is Arabic, but teaching at the university is in English. *Member, United Nations.*

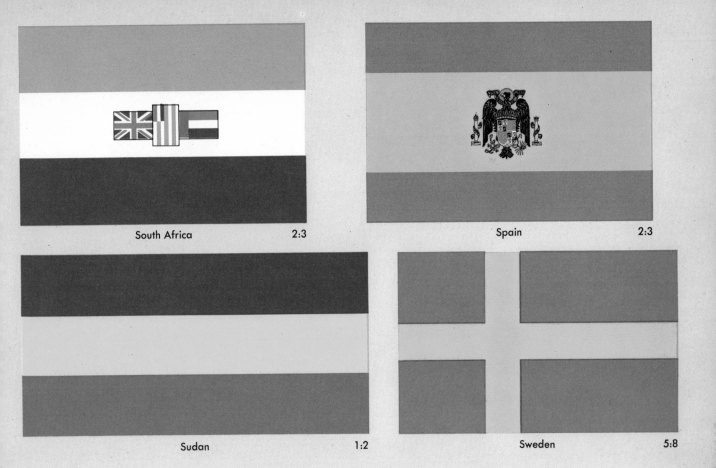

South Africa   2:3

Spain   2:3

Sudan   1:2

Sweden   5:8

SWEDEN (SWEE-den): From A.D. 800 to 1050, the men called vikings spread outward from Sweden, just as they did from Norway. Swedish vikings went eastward, far into Russia and even beyond to Moslem countries in Central Asia and the Near East. These early pagan warriors flew their own flag, but the flag of modern Sweden had its origin in Christian tradition.

All over Europe in the Middle Ages it was common for Christians to believe that they would get help from God if they carried a banner with a cross on it. Sometimes in a war both sides had such a banner. After the Swedes became Christians, they followed this general custom. By the middle of the seventeenth century they had come to regard the yellow cross on a blue field as the symbol of their country. After 1814, when Sweden and Norway united, details of the flag changed several times, but it always kept the cross. Then the two countries separated in 1905, and Sweden adopted the form it still uses.

In 1906, government officials sent out samples of blue cloth which were to be used as guides whenever flags were manufactured. It happens that blue dye is very likely to fade slowly with age, and so the color of the Swedish flag changed little by little over the years, as manufacturers kept checking their dyes against aging samples. Finally, someone real-

A young Swedish girl.

ized that the blue had become much lighter than it was originally intended to be. An official formula has now been worked out to make sure that future flags will be accurately colored.

The Kingdom of Sweden is a constitutional monarchy. Most of its 8,000,000 people speak Swedish, which is closely related to Danish and Norwegian. A few thousand Swedish-born descendants of Finns keep their own language, and there are about 30,000 Finnish-speaking Lapps, some of whom live as nomadic reindeer herders. Unlike the blond Swedes and Finns, the Lapps are short and dark and they look very Mongolian. Long ago, they gave up their own language and changed to Finnish, although the two peoples are not related.

All religions are permitted in Sweden, but the Lutheran State Church has official government recognition and is supported by taxes. *Member, United Nations.*

SWITZERLAND: When this land of forests and glaciers was part of the Roman Empire, the Swiss apparently spoke a form of Latin. Then German tribes came down from the north, and some of the Latin-speaking people were driven out. Others fled into two high mountain valleys. There nobody bothered them. So they kept their language, which gradually changed, as all languages do. Now it is called Romansh, and about 50,000 descendants of those early refugees use it.

Switzerland has four official languages—Romansh, German, French

128

and Italian—because it is in fact a union of many mountain-valley communities with a long history of cooperation in defending their freedom. Its official name is the Swiss Confederation.

For more than seven hundred years a white cross on a red background has been a familiar flag in Switzerland. It was well known in 1648, when most of the country became independent of the Holy Roman Empire (see GERMANY). It was made the official Swiss flag in 1848, but the present shape of the cross—with its four equal arms, did not appear until later. The International Red Cross Organization, which began in Switzerland and has its headquarters there, adopted a flag that was just the reverse of the Swiss flag—a white background and a cross of red.

Altogether there are about 6,000,000 Swiss. The majority are Protestants, but there is freedom of religion for the large group of Roman Catholics and for a small number who follow other faiths or none. Switzerland makes no military treaties with other countries, and it is the home of several international organizations, including some connected with the United Nations. But Switzerland itself does not belong to the United Nations.

Switzerland: Tossing the national flag to the music of an Alpine horn is men's sport.

SYRIA (SEER-yuh): Damascus, capital of Syria, is one of the oldest cities in the world. It was already ancient when, in the seventh century A.D., it became the center of the Arab empire. At other times, Syria has been ruled by other foreign conquerors, including Crusaders from Europe and Mongols from Asia. It was part of the Turkish Empire from 1516 until the end of World War I. Then France took over control and ruled until January 1, 1944, when Syria became fully independent.

In 1958, Syria joined Egypt in the United Arab Republic, and the two countries adopted a flag like the one still used by Egypt (see UNITED ARAB REPUBLIC). A short time later, Iraq began to consider joining the union and plans were made for a flag with three stars to stand for the close relationship of the three countries. In the end, Syria withdrew from the union, becoming the Syrian Arab Republic, and Iraq did not join. Both countries, however, adopted the same new flag, with its three stars, in 1963.

Syria has given its own symbolic meaning to the flag. The three stars now stand for Arab revolutions. The colors green, white and black stand for three groups of ancient Moslem leaders (see page 10).

The majority of the 5,500,000 Syrians are Moslems, but there are also many Christians among them. The official language is Arabic. Armenians who live in Syria keep their own language, and there are still villages near Damascus where people speak Aramaic, which was the language of Jesus. *Member, United Nations.*

TANZANIA (tan-zan-EE-uh): The oldest fossilized human bones ever found come from Tanganyika, which is part of Tanzania. This means that the human race may have begun there more than 2,000,000 years ago. If this is so, the very new country of Tanzania has a longer human story than any other country in the world.

Arabs began to settle in Tanganyika in the eighth century, but for more than a thousand years the country remained the home of independent tribes. Germany seized part of it in 1885, but lost it in World War I. The British ruled after that, until Tanganyika became independent in 1961.

Zanzibar, also part of Tanzania, is an island off the coast of Africa. The Portuguese ruled it from about 1500 to about 1700. Arabs from the Sultanate of Muscat then ruled until 1856, when Zanzibar became independent under the rule of its own sultan. In 1890, by agreement among the big European countries, Britain added Zanzibar to its colonial empire.

The island again became an independent sultanate in 1963, but a revolution overthrew the sultan in 1964. Later that year, Zanzibar and Tanganyika united, forming Tanzania. In the flag that was adopted,

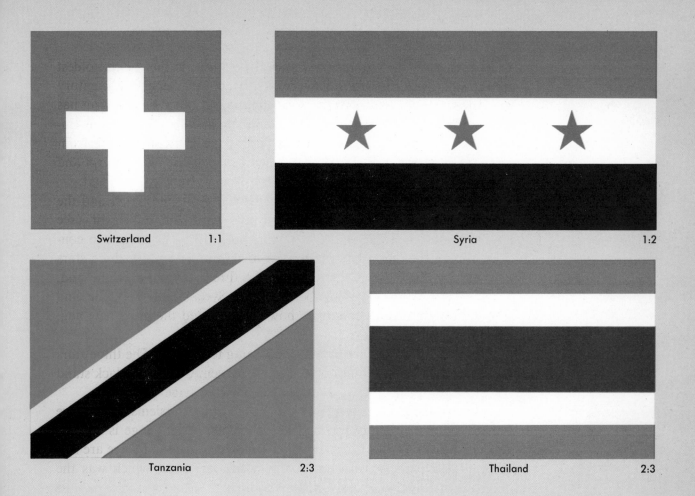

Switzerland 1:1

Syria 1:2

Tanzania 2:3

Thailand 2:3

black stands for the people; green is for the land; yellow is for the country's wealth; blue represents the sea.

Over 10,000,000 people in the United Republic of Tanzania belong to about 125 tribes with almost as many languages and dialects. The intertribal language called Swahili is official, and both Swahili and English are taught in the schools. About half of the people practice tribal religions. The next largest group are Moslems and there are many Christians, Buddhists, Hindus and members of other Asian sects. *Member, United Nations.*

THAILAND (TIE-land): Until about 200 B.C. the Thai people lived in southern China. Then they began to move out, and they kept moving for hundreds of years. A great many of them settled in what is now called Thailand. There an independent kingdom grew up, and the country never became a colony of any of the European powers. Thais call their country "Land of the Free." They also call it "Land of the Elephant." Among foreigners it was once known as Siam.

Two-thirds of the 31,000,000 people are descendants of the ancient emigrants from China. They use the Thai language, which is required

Thailand: A canoe on a tributary of the Mekong River.

in all of the schools. There are also a great many Chinese who arrived more recently, and they continue to use Chinese as well as Thai. A small number of Malays keep their own language. Buddhism is the national faith, but Moslems, Christians and others have freedom to worship.

The white in the flag, which was adopted in 1917, stands for the Buddhist faith. Red represents the nation, and blue stands for the monarchy. Until 1932 the king had absolute power. Now he governs under a constitution. King Rama IX, who came to the throne in 1946, was born while his parents were living in the United States. He grew up to like Occidental music and learned to play the clarinet and saxophone. *Member, United Nations.*

TOGO (TOE-go): Although there are only about 1,800,000 people in Togo, they are divided into thirteen main tribes. Each has its own religion and language, but many people also speak Hausa, the language of a tribe that does not live in Togo.

When countries in Europe began to rule different parts of Africa,

132

A mother learns how to write in an adult-education class, Togo.

the long, narrow strip of land now called the Republic of Togo came under the control of Germany. During World War I, Germany lost the colony, and after 1922 France ruled it. In 1960, Togo became independent.

Togolese tell two stories about the symbolism of the flag they have adopted. One is this: the green stands for hope and for agriculture (about 90 per cent of the Togolese are farmers); yellow stands for faith in the importance of their work; red is the color of charity, faithfulness, love and sacrifice for humanity; white is the symbol of purity.

In the other explanation of the colors, yellow is said to stand for mineral resources, red is to remind everyone of the blood shed in the struggle for independence, and the white star means hope. *Member, United Nations.*

133

TONGA (TONG-gah): The Kingdom of Tonga is a group of about two hundred small islands in the South Pacific. When Captain James Cook visited them nearly two hundred years ago, he named them the Friendly Islands, although their people did not make him especially welcome. The greatest of their leaders was King George Tubou I, who brought agreement among various tribes, united the islands in 1845, and ruled under a constitution for almost fifty years. The great nations respected him and several made treaties with him guaranteeing Tonga's independence. Since 1900, the country's foreign affairs have been handled by Britain.

The 71,000 Tongans are, for the most part, Christians. They speak Tongan, a Polynesian language, but laws are printed in English, which many people speak. All children must go to school till they are fourteen, and education is free. Although there are no real newspapers, the government prints and distributes a free daily news bulletin.

The cross on the flag means that the islands are Christian; the red is for the blood Jesus shed on the cross.

TRINIDAD (TRIN-ih-dad) **AND TOBAGO** (toh-BAY-go): When Columbus came ashore on the island of Trinidad in 1498, he hoisted the Royal Standard of Ferdinand and Isabella and claimed the land for Spain. The Spanish flag continued to fly there for almost a hundred years. During that period the Dutch, French and British tried at various times to claim the island, along with the neighboring island of Tobago. The British won. After 1797, Britain ruled both islands until 1962, when independence came to the 1,000,000 English-speaking Trinidadians. (That is what the inhabitants of both islands are now called.)

The national flag was designed by a committee of the government and is full of symbolic meanings. Its unusual design represents independence. Black stands for the devotion of Trinidadians to national unity. White stands for the sea around the islands, for the purity of the people's hopes and for the equality of all men. Red is for the vitality of the people and of their land. It also stands for friendliness and for the warmth and energy of the sun.

Almost half of the Trinidadians are Negro. More than one-third are East Indian. The remainder are of Lebanese, Syrian, European and Chinese origin. About 70 per cent are Christians, evenly divided between Roman Catholics and Protestants. The others are Hindus and Moslems. *Member, United Nations.*

TRUCIAL (TRU-shull) **STATES:** These seven small states, also known as Trucial Oman, or the Trucial Sheikdoms or the Trucial Coast, stretch for four hundred miles along the coast of Arabia from the border of Qatar to Muscat and Oman. Each state has a separate treaty with Britain, and all are bound together by a treaty among themselves, with

Togo   2:3

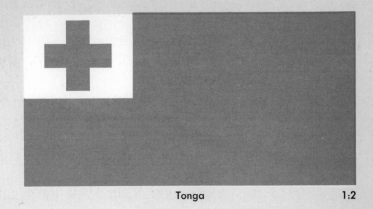

Tonga   1:2

Trinidad and Tobago   3:5

Trucial States (Ajman and Dubai)   1:4

Britain as an eighth party. Under these agreements, Britain has the right to conduct their foreign relations, but in other matters they act independently.

The people of the Trucial Coast have a long history as fishermen and pearl divers, and their *dhows,* a special kind of Arab sailing vessel, once carried sea traders all around the Persian Gulf and the Arabian Sea. About 150 years ago they turned to piracy. Their dhows began to use the red flag that was common to all the states along the Gulf, and the area became known as the Pirate Coast. After some British ships were raided, the British navy attacked and forced the states, in 1820, to sign a peace treaty. This was followed, in 1853, by another agreement called a maritime truce, which pledged the states not to commit piracy or wage war on the seas. In return, Britain promised to protect them from sea

135

attack by other powers. From this truce came the name Trucial States.

Each of the states, Abu Dhabi, Umm al Quiwain, Ajman, Dubai, Sharjah, Ras al Khaimah and Fujairah, is ruled by its own sheik, or chieftain. Altogether, about 115,000 people live along the Trucial Coast, about half of them in Abu Dhabi, and most are Moslems. The official language is Arabic.

Each of the seven flags is some variant of the old solid red flag (see page 10). Fujairah keeps it without any emblems or change. All the others have some white in them, either as a canton (Abu Dhabi), a vertical white stripe at the hoist (Ajman and Dubai), the traditional Moslem symbol of crescent and star in the center (Umm al Quiwain), or as a white border (Sharjah and Ras al Khaimah). The white was added to these flags by agreement with Britain, so that friendly Arab vessels could be distinguished from pirate ships. Since Fujairah was not one of the states that originally signed the truce, it did not have to use white in its flag.

TUNISIA (too-NIZ-yuh): Nearly three thousand years ago, merchants and mariners from Phoenicia along the eastern shore of the Mediterranean Sea built the city of Carthage on the north coast of Africa in what is now Tunisia. These Phoenicians are said to have brought with them two emblems, the crescent and the star. About 2,500 years later, when flags had come to be widely used, a certain Spanish friar observed the crescent on the flags of two cities in Tunisia (see page 13). In Mahdia, the Moslem king used a purple crescent on a white field. In Tunis, "a great and rich city, well supplied with all things," said the friar, the king flew a white flag with a black moon in the shape of a crescent. There were similar flags along the coast of North Africa at that time, but nobody knows whether the crescent had been in use ever since Phoenician times or whether it had been borrowed from the flags of Moslem rulers in Damascus and Cairo, both of whom also had moons on their flags in the fourteenth century.

Still later, when Turkey conquered Tunisia, the crescent appeared again. This time it was on the flag of the Ottoman Empire, which was red. And for the last eighty years or so of Turkish rule, the flag had a star on it, as well as a crescent.

After 1881, Tunisia was part of the French Empire—until 1956, when it gained independence and adopted a constitution that is similar in many ways to that of the United States. At the same time the traditional red flag was retained to remind Tunisians of their long history.

Soon after Tunisia became a separate nation, each of its nearly 5,000,000 inhabitants received a family name. Until then, most of them had never had names that identified them very clearly. A man might be called Mohammed ben Ahmed ben Mohammed, but that is only a way of saying that he was Mohammed, the son of Ahmed who was the son of Mohammed. A law requiring family names went into effect in 1959.

After independence, Arabic became the official language of the government and the schools. However, some French is still taught. In 1885, when Tunisia was under Turkish rule, only 732 boys and six girls attended schools. Two years after independence, 230,000 boys and 110,000 girls were in public schools, and the number is still growing. *Member, United Nations.*

TURKEY: Far back in ancient times, no one knows just when, a group of related tribes began to make their homes in Central Asia and Siberia. From there they went on raids westward toward Europe, looking for wealth. Apparently they were proud warriors, for they called themselves the Strong People. In their languages the word for *strong* or *strength* was *turk,* so all of their tribes came to be called *Turkic.* In the seventh century A.D., the westernmost of the Turkic peoples began to meet the Moslem missionary armies from Arabia, and before long the raiders were moving in the direction of the Arab lands. When the Moslem officers saw the fierce ability of these Turks, they decided it would be better to hire such warriors than to fight them. So Turks began to enter the armies of Islam, and the Islamic faith spread among their whole tribe. The tribe itself grew and settled down in the area between the Black Sea and the Mediterranean.

At first there were many small Turkish principalities. Then, in 1288, one leader named Osman (or Othman) united most of them. His descendants, called Osmanlis or Ottomans, ruled as sultans for nearly 650 years over a large territory known as the Ottoman Empire or Ottoman Turkey. In the seventeenth century, Ottoman sultans controlled everything from Yemen in the south to Hungary in the north, and from Morocco in the west to Iran in the east.

Businessmen commute to work on a ferry, Istanbul, Turkey.

At one time, the conquering Turkish soldiers went to war for a sultan who used the black flag which was called the Flag of the Prophet, meaning Mohammed. Various divisions among the troops had their own banners, some of which bore two horses' tails, some three. No one seems to know just when the Turks began to use a red flag. They could have seen it among other Moslems as early as the seventh century when the Kharijite sect began to fly a red flag in the eastern part of the growing Moslem world (see page 10). Nor is it known when the Turks added a crescent moon to their flag, but one thing is certain — they did not invent the crescent. It had been around for a long time. Ancient Egyptians carved it on statues of the moon goddess. Moon-worshipers in the Euphrates Valley had used it as early as 1900 B.C. A crescent with a star was a symbol of the city of Byzantium (now called Istanbul), founded in the seventh century B.C. Arabs had found the same symbol in the seventh century A.D. when they captured Harran, a city of moon-worshipers near the present border of Syria and Turkey.

It seems fairly definite that the Turks added a star to their flag about 1798. Authorities disagree on what it stood for. Some say it represented Thrace, the part of Turkey which lies in Europe. Regardless of what it originally meant, the star — like the crescent — has become a popular Moslem emblem throughout the world.

The Turks still ruled over a large but decaying empire at the beginning of World War I, when they were allies of the Germans. At the end of the war, Turkey's former possessions had either become independent or were taken over by other countries. Finally, after a revolution in 1923, the Ottoman sultanate ended, and the Republic of Turkey was established.

A red flag with a white crescent and star continues to fly over the country's 31,500,000 people, about 85 per cent of whom are Turks. The rest are Kurds, Arabs, Armenians, Georgians, Greeks, Bulgarians and Circassians, each group with its own language. Less than one per cent of the total population are Christians; most of the others are Moslems. About 40,000 Jews speak a language called Spaniol or Ladino, a mixture of fifteenth-century Spanish, Hebrew, Arabic and Turkish. The people who use it are descended from Jews who were expelled from Spain in 1492, when the Christians finally won control there. *Member, United Nations.*

UGANDA (yoo-GAHN-da): The people in Uganda like to say that this beautiful and varied country is "The Pearl of Africa." One of its borders is a ridge of volcanoes called the Mountains of the Moon. Another is Lake Victoria, second largest lake in the world and source of the Nile River. Although the country lies across the Equator, there are glaciers on its very high peaks.

The 7,600,000 Ugandans are themselves as varied as their country. Each of the many tribes has its own customs and language. Members of the different tribes seldom intermarry. Twelve of their languages have been written down, and there are daily radio programs in ten of them. Luganda is the most widely spoken. Swahili is also well-known. Kings, whose powers are limited by a constitution, rule in different districts, but the country as a whole is a republic and has a president. It became independent in 1962.

In the latter part of the nineteenth century, after Britain took over control of Uganda, Protestant, Catholic and Moslem missionaries all made converts among the people, and religious competition became keen. In 1892, there was a serious battle between Catholics and Protestants. At the time when the country became independent, about half the Ugandans were Christians of one kind or another; about 300,000

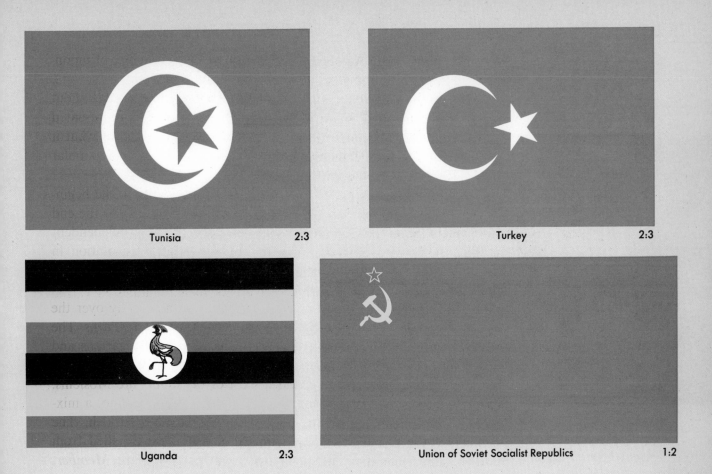

Tunisia   2:3

Turkey   2:3

Uganda   2:3

Union of Soviet Socialist Republics   1:2

were Moslems and the remainder were divided among many tribal religions.

From time to time, some of the tribes have also fought each other in disputes over laws, taxes or control of land. One of the new government's biggest tasks is the creation of uniform laws for people who have so many different rules and customs.

A crested crane, used as a symbol for Uganda while it was a British colony, was put on the flag when the country won independence. *Member, United Nations.*

UNION OF SOVIET SOCIALIST REPUBLICS: Perhaps in the fifth century, European tribesmen known as Slavs began to settle on the borders of a great forest that covered most of Russia. In the ninth century, vikings began to travel through this land where the Slavs had settled. Travel from the Baltic Sea in the north to the Black Sea in the south was not too difficult for the seafaring Norsemen, because a long chain of lakes and rivers covered most of the way. To protect this trade route, the vikings themselves had settlements. One was at Kiev on the Dnieper River, and it became the center of the first Russian state. The first ruler there, according to tradition, was a viking named Rurik, and

139

A Soviet scientist records the sounds of a chimpanzee for a study in vocal reactions.

the men who ruled Russia for hundreds of years all claimed to be descended from him.

During the thirteenth and fourteenth centuries, Mongol invaders from Asia controlled much of Russia. Then the Russians drove the Mongols out and began to conquer an empire for themselves, all the way eastward to the Pacific Ocean.

In 1917, before the end of World War I, a revolution overthrew the emperor who was called the *czar.* In the cities, Russian workers formed committees or councils, called *soviets,* which took control of the government. Soon the Communist Party began to direct the Soviets, and in 1922 the new government chose the name Union of Soviet Socialist Republics. The country was called a union because in it were united many separate nationalities which set up socialist republics in various parts of the old empire.

Most people in the Russian Republic speak Russian, as do a good many in all the other republics. There are about one hundred languages altogether in the U.S.S.R., each spoken by a separate nationality. School children study in the language of their own nationality, and they also learn Russian.

Christianity had entered Russia by A.D. 988. Most Russians became members of the Eastern Orthodox Church, but other Christian denominations gained members, and eight still exist. There are also Moslems, Jews and Buddhists. All are allowed to hold services, although the government is atheistic. Apparently about one-tenth of the 235,000,000 Soviet citizens consider themselves religious.

In 1923, the new Soviet government adopted the red flag (see page 15) as the national flag. A hammer in the canton stands for workers, a sickle for peasants. Above them a five-pointed star represents the unity of the working people of the five continents (Europe and Asia being counted as one). *Member, United Nations.*

UNITED ARAB REPUBLIC: Much of modern civilization began on the banks of the Nile River, which every year overflows and leaves new rich soil on a strip of land that runs through the Egyptian desert.

More than five thousand years ago Egyptians were raising crops on this fertile soil, and with a reliable food supply, they found time and energy to develop arts and sciences and their own system of writing. (The latter idea had come to them from Sumer, another agricultural area which lay between the Tigris and Euphrates Rivers of Iraq.)

Egyptian farming also supported kings and the armies which carried their standards into battle. Later, Roman armies under Julius Caesar brought their own standards when they conquered Egypt, but neither the Egyptians nor the Romans used true flags. Nor did the early Christians when their religion spread into the valley of the Nile. Flags did begin to appear when Arab armies arrived in the seventh century A.D., bringing the Islamic faith and the Arabic language.

Arabic still remains the tongue of the 29,000,000 Egyptians, about 90 per cent of whom are Moslems. Less than 8 per cent are Christians, some of them belonging to sects that are very old but not widespread. The majority of people are descendants of ancient Egyptians and are often called Fellahin. Jews, Bedouins and dark-skinned Numidians make up small groups in the population.

After the days of the Arab invasion, the Turks, the French, and finally the British sent troops into Egypt. In 1922, the country became an independent monarchy that kept close ties with Britain. In 1953, the monarchy was abolished and a republic established. Five years later, Egypt and Syria joined to form the United Arab Republic.

The flag adopted in 1958 had two green stars representing Egypt and Syria. The red stripe, they decided, would represent the revolutions in which both countries had established republics. The white was for peace and prosperity, and the black stood for the dark past. These are all modern meanings attached to colors that have long had religious significance in the Moslem world (see page 10).

In 1961, Syria withdrew from the union, but Egypt continued to call itself the United Arab Republic and to use the two-starred flag. *Member, United Nations.*

A camel turns a water wheel for irrigation in the Nile Valley of Egypt.

UNITED KINGDOM: Three separate stories lie behind the flag of the United Kingdom. One begins with a legend about a certain soldier named George who served under the Roman Emperor Diocletian around the year 300. George was converted to the Christian religion against the wishes of the Emperor, who ordered his head cut off. Because George suffered death for his belief, he was made a saint. At the time of the Crusades, many English knights prayed to this soldier-saint before they entered battle. The English warriors fared so well in some of their combats that they came to regard St. George as a kind of special protector. Through custom, a red cross on a white background became a symbol for St. George, and many knights wore it on coats that covered their armor. In fact, so many wore it that by the year 1277 the cross of St. George had become an English national emblem.

The second story behind the British flag begins with a legend from the Greek island of Patras. There, in A.D. 69, a man named Andrew was tied to an X-shaped cross and killed because he had become a Christian. Some friends who shared Andrew's belief preserved his bones and put them in a monastery. Three hundred years later, a vision came to one of the monks—ordering him to take some of Andrew's bones and sail with them over the sea, far to the west. This monk was shipwrecked on the shore of Scotland, where the Scots let him build a church that is called St. Andrew's to this day. Gradually the Scottish people began to regard St. Andrew as a special protector of their country, and they adopted as a national flag his special X-shaped cross, made in white in a blue field.

The third strand in the story also has to do with a saint, a Scot who took the name Patricius and went to Ireland as a missionary. He brought many Irishmen into the Christian church, and a red cross in the form of an X became associated with his name. In time, Patricius came to be known as St. Patrick, protector of Ireland.

In 1603, England and Scotland were united, and King James I ordered ships to fly a flag that combined the English cross of St. George with the Scottish cross of St. Andrew. In 1801, the cross of St. Patrick was added to the flag, showing that Ireland had been united with Scotland and England. (Wales had already been absorbed by England, and its flag had not been included.) The southern part of Ireland became independent in 1922, so now the United Kingdom includes only Northern Ireland, England, Scotland and Wales. Its official name is the United Kingdom of Great Britain and Northern Ireland.

A series of different tribes moved into the British Isles after the end of the Ice Age. Because one of them was called the Angles and another the Saxons, English people are sometimes still called Anglo-Saxons. Descendants of the tribes called Celts live mainly in Scotland, Wales and Ireland. In Scotland, a few thousand people still speak Scots-Gaelic, a Celtic language, and there are people in Northern Ireland who speak an Irish dialect of Gaelic. In Wales, both Welsh and English are taught in the schools. English is the official language of the United Kingdom.

Between the end of the sixteenth century and the early twentieth century, Britain built up a vast empire with colonies and possessions all over the world. In 1931, several of Britain's former Dominions joined with the United Kingdom as equal partners in the Commonwealth of Nations.

The Church of England (also called Anglican) is the official church of the country, and the government appoints bishops, archbishops and other dignitaries. Half of the 54,500,000 people in the United Kingdom are members of the church. The remainder belong to various Christian denominations or follow other faiths. There are nearly half a million Jews. *Member, United Nations.*

UNITED STATES OF AMERICA: In the eighteenth century, before the United States became an independent country, a large British business organization, the East India Company, flew its own private flag of red, white and blue. This flag had the British Union Flag in the canton; the rest of it consisted of seven red and six white stripes — thirteen in all. Apparently, these thirteen stripes caught the attention of someone in

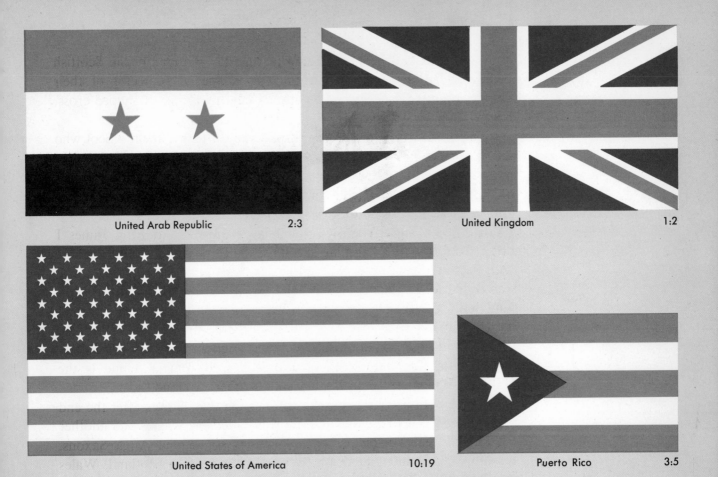

United Arab Republic   2:3

United Kingdom   1:2

United States of America   10:19

Puerto Rico   3:5

New England at the time when the thirteen American colonies were beginning to rebel against injustices in British rule. Why not make it the regular flag of the colonies? It had the additional advantage of including the British flag, and Americans felt an attachment to the country from which many of their ancestors had come. So the East India Company flag served as a model for one that the American Continental Army used for a while. It was first raised over the headquarters of General George Washington near Boston in January, 1776.

After the colonies decided to declare their independence, members of the Continental Congress agreed that the British flag should be left out of the banner under which they would fight against Britain. In its place, Congress put thirteen white stars in a blue field. This was a way of saying that a new group of states had come into the world, just as a new constellation might appear in the sky. The thirteen red-and-white East India Company stripes remained. Thus the United States flag grew by stages out of earlier British flags, just as the country itself had grown out of British colonies.

A legend says that a seamstress named Betsy Ross made the first Stars and Stripes. There is no proof for this story, which may have been started by one of Betsy Ross' descendants.

Football fans watching a game, Philadelphia, Pa., U.S.A.

By 1812, the flag had fifteen stars and fifteen stripes—one for each state in the expanding country. A fifteen-stripe flag, a huge one forty-two feet long and thirty feet high, flew over a fort that was attacked by the British in the War of 1812. This was the Star-Spangled Banner which, in 1814, inspired Francis Scott Key to write the song that became the national anthem of the United States. In 1818, the design of the flag was revised. It went back to thirteen stripes, one for each of the original colonies. But it kept the canton with a blue field, and in it the white stars—one for each state in the Union. The fiftieth star, which stands for Hawaii, was added in 1960. All the states and the District of Columbia have flags of their own. So have these United States possessions: Guam, the Virgin Islands, American Samoa and the United States Trust Territory of the Pacific Islands. Puerto Ricans, who are United States citizens, have a flag for their Commonwealth which closely resembles the flag of Cuba. It was adopted by revolutionaries in 1895, when Puerto Ricans, like the Cubans, were seeking independence from Spain.

About one-tenth of the 200,000,000 people in the United States have Negro ancestors who were brought from Africa as slaves. Nearly nine-tenths are descended from immigrants who came from one of the countries of Europe. About 750,000 are of Asian origin. American Indians number a little over half a million, and some of them still speak one of a number of Indian languages. English, however, is the official language of the country as a whole. In the Commonwealth of Puerto Rico, Spanish is the main language of the people. It is also the tongue of many in New Mexico, where it is legally recognized, along with English.

The United States has no official religion, and church and state are separate. About two-thirds of the population are church members. About 70,000,000 are Protestants, about 46,000,000 Catholics, and about 5,600,000 Jews. There are also small groups who follow all the other world faiths, and many Indians practice their own tribal religions. *Member, United Nations.*

144

UPPER VOLTA: In the twelfth century A.D., a strong feudal state grew up on the plains of West Africa. Its monarch, who was worshiped as a symbol of the sun-come-down-to-earth, ruled with the help of four chiefs. One was in charge of the palace, one in charge of the royal tombs, and the other two commanded the infantry and the cavalry. The whole state was so strictly organized as a military unit that many of the people still remain, after eight hundred years, a disciplined group with very little individual freedom.

Since the twelfth century, their rulers have changed more than once. Part of their land was for a while in the Moslem Empire of Mali, and there are still many Moslems among them, as well as followers of tribal religions. Much later, in 1897, France took control of the area.

Two main groups of those earlier tribes remain in what is now the Upper Volta Republic, and they make up most of the country's 5,000,000 people. Within each group several languages are spoken. In addition, there are Hausa-speaking merchants who travel around the country, colorful Moslem horsemen called Tuaregs, and about 200,000 members of the wandering Fulani tribe who act as herders for cattle owned by other people who stay at home and spend their time farming.

Three main branches of the Volta River run through the country, giving it not only its name but also the colors in its flag. Black is for the Black Volta, white for the White Volta and red for the Red Volta. The flag was adopted in 1959, before the establishment of independence, which came in 1960. Because the French had ruled the country for more than sixty years, the official language remains French. Half of all the Upper Voltans are under twenty years of age, but only a small number of these young people have had a chance to go to school. *Member, United Nations.*

URUGUAY (YOUR-uh-gwigh): Together with its neighbor Argentina, Uruguay was once part of a Spanish colony along the Uruguay River, and beginning in 1811, the two regions shared in the fight to win freedom from Spain. Afterward, when Uruguayans wanted to have their own separate government, they had to struggle first against Argentina, then against Portuguese invaders from Brazil, and they did not finally achieve full independence until 1828. At that time Uruguay adopted a white flag with nine blue stripes, representing its nine departments, or states, and a golden sun in the canton. Two years later, the flag was changed to its present form—four blue stripes and five white ones. The colors are the same as those of the Argentine state flag, and the sun is similar. Both the sun and the colors have their beginnings in the legend of the "Sun of May," which is told earlier in this book (see ARGENTINA). In the Uruguayan flag, of course, the sun symbolizes the independence of Uruguay.

Almost all of the 3,000,000 people who live in Uruguay are descended from Europeans who came as settlers from Spain, Italy, France and Switzerland. Only a handful have mixed Spanish and Indian ancestors. Most Uruguayans who go to church are Roman Catholics, but the country is not strongly religious, and it allows complete freedom of worship. The language is Spanish. Since Uruguay was originally the eastern part of the old Spanish colony, its name in Spanish means the "Republic East of the Uruguay [River]." In English the official name is The Oriental (meaning Eastern) Republic of Uruguay. *Member, United Nations.*

VATICAN (VAT-ih-can) **CITY:** In the words of the Gospel according to Matthew, in the Christian Bible, Jesus said to his disciple Peter, "I will give you the keys of the kingdom of heaven." Among Christians the belief grew that there were two of these keys to heaven: one was silver, the other gold. A French leader of the First Crusade named Godfrey of Bouillon remembered this in 1099, the year when other Crusaders chose him to be ruler over the recently captured city of Jerusalem. Godfrey chose a flag made of silver and gold, the colors of the keys to heaven. Later, the popes of the Roman Catholic Church borrowed Godfrey's colors for the flag they used as rulers of the Papal States in Italy, reminding Roman Catholics of their belief that popes receive their authority from Jesus through St. Peter.

In the early nineteenth century, the popes ruled over 3,000,000 people in the Papal States that stretched across the center of Italy. When Italians later united to support one government for the whole country, the Papal States disappeared. Then, in 1929, when Mussolini was dictator of Italy, the independent State of Vatican City was established. It adopted the old flag of the Papal States — white and yellow, with the crossed keys of St. Peter, and above them the crown a pope wears.

This flag is the only one in Europe which has white next to yellow (silver next to gold). Other countries follow the ancient rule of heraldry that the two metals should not be placed side by side.

Vatican City covers about 109 acres in the center of Rome. About a thousand people are citizens of the state, which conducts its business in Italian while the religious business of the Roman Catholic Church has traditionally been conducted in Latin. In Vatican City are the largest church and the largest palace in the world, one of the world's greatest libraries, several important museums of art and archeology, an astronomical observatory, a shop that can do printing in many languages, a radio station, and a railroad station. Vatican City has its own coins and stamps, and it has its own little army called the Swiss Guards—Catholics from Switzerland who wear medieval uniforms said to have been designed by Michelangelo.

146

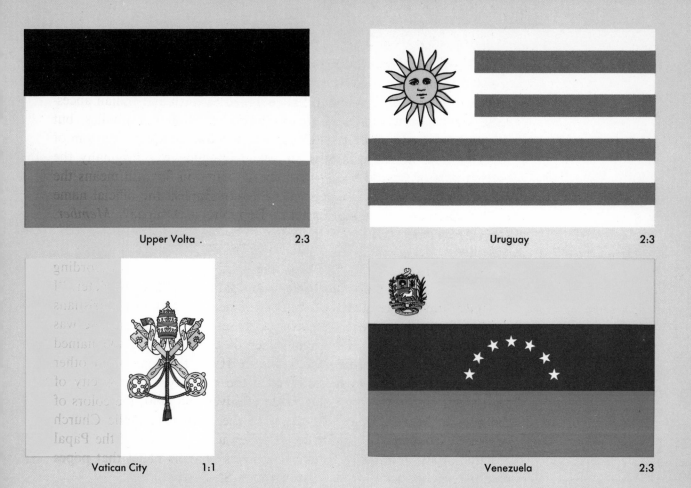

Upper Volta . 2:3

Uruguay 2:3

Vatican City 1:1

Venezuela 2:3

VENEZUELA (venne-ZWAY-luh): About ten years after the American Revolution, a young Venezuelan named Francisco Miranda visited the United States. Miranda believed the time had come for Spain's colonies to revolt, and he asked George Washington, Alexander Hamilton, Thomas Paine and others for help. The leaders of the United States were afraid to give it. They could not afford to risk a war with Spain so soon after their long war with Britain. So they had to tell Miranda that they were sorry, but they could not let him have the money and weapons he needed.

Miranda traveled to France and fought in the French Revolution. In 1806, he went home and tried unsuccessfully to lead a revolt there. Later he met Simón Bolívar, another Venezuelan who shared his ideas about freedom and democracy. The two men decided they must try again. When they reached Venezuela in 1811, they found that an uprising had already started. Miranda became a leader, but this rebellion, too, failed, and the Spaniards captured him. He died in prison. Bolívar was more fortunate. He went on to lead so many victorious armies in several countries that people called him "The Liberator."

When Venezuela became completely independent of Spain in 1824,

147

the people honored Miranda by adopting the flag which he had designed and which Bolívar had carried in battle. Like the flag of the French Revolution, it had — and still has — three stripes, but one is yellow instead of white. (The Venezuelan colors are the same as those of Colombia and Ecuador, because all three nations were for a while united in a country known as *Gran Colombia*.) Seven stars in the blue stripe remind Venezuelans that seven provinces signed their Declaration of Independence in 1810. The coat of arms in the yellow stripe contains symbols for wealth, unity, victory in battle, and liberty.

Most of the 9,000,000 Venezuelans belong to the Roman Catholic Church. A tiny minority who have pure Indian ancestors practice their own religions and speak their own languages. The majority, who are of mixed Spanish and Indian descent, speak Spanish. So do a small number of Negroes. *Member, United Nations.*

Men dressed as devils parade ceremonially from church to police station to hold court, Venezuela.

VIETNAM (vee-ETT-nam): More than two thousand years ago, some people known as Viets were driven out of central China and settled in Southeast Asia. Even in the new land, the Viets continued to be under Chinese rule. But in A.D. 939 they drove out the Chinese, and during the next thousand years (off and on) they managed to control much of the area now known as Vietnam. In the nineteenth century, the French began a rule that lasted until 1941, when Japan occupied the country. The Japanese, in 1945, set up a government headed by Emperor Bao Dai which adopted a flag with a design of red horizontal bars in a yellow field.

After Japan was defeated in World War II, the French tried to take back their former territory in Southeast Asia. They gave support to Bao Dai, but were opposed by revolutionists who, in 1945, had announced the formation of the Democratic Republic of Vietnam, adopted a flag, and declared their independence of both Bao Dai and the French. For the next nine years there was continuous warfare. By 1954, the French had been defeated, and a peace agreement was signed in Geneva, Switzerland, providing for the temporary division of Vietnam into two parts — one in the north and one in the south. The northern part, which was governed by communists, kept the name Democratic Republic of Vietnam and, in 1955, adopted the 1945 flag which is still in use. The red stands for revolution; the five points of the star symbolize five sections of the population: peasants, workers, intellectuals, young people and soldiers.

In the southern part of the country, in 1948, a new state was established, with Bao Dai as emperor and a flag which grew out of the one Bao Dai had used under the Japanese. It had the same yellow field, and its three horizontal stripes resembled the former red bars, except that they were lengthened. This flag continued in use after Bao Dai was overthrown in 1955 and the Republic of Vietnam was established. It remains the flag of South Vietnam today. Meantime, the United States, which had begun to send military men to advise Bao Dai in 1950, continued to supply military advisers to the Republic of Vietnam.

On December 20, 1960, there appeared in South Vietnam a new organization which had as its aim the expulsion of the Americans and the overthrow of the American-supported South Vietnamese government. This organization called itself the National Liberation Front of South Vietnam (N.L.F.). It established an army known as the Vietcong and adopted a flag similar to that of North Vietnam, except that it was half blue and half red. N.L.F. officials say that the blue stands for peace, and it is also said to represent a group of tribesmen called Montagnards.

The population of North Vietnam is about 18,500,000; of South Vietnam, about 15,375,000. By 1968 there were also in South Vietnam about 400,000 military men from the United States and about 50,000 from South Korea. In both parts of the country the Viet people are the majority, but there are more than forty minority groups, each with its own language or dialect. Vietnamese is the official language in both North and South. Buddhists are the largest religious group; there are also followers of the Roman Catholic, Protestant, Hoa Hao, Cao-Daist and Binh-Xuyen religions.

School children study with help of tape recorder, Western Samoa.

WESTERN SAMOA (sah-MOH-uh): Polynesian explorers reached the volcanic islands of Western Samoa about 1000 B.C. The first Europeans visited there in A.D. 1722, and in 1830, a Christian missionary from England came to stay. After that, England, the United States and Germany all did trading in the islands. Then, in 1899, Germany began to rule Western Samoa, and a year later the United States took control of Eastern Samoa. New Zealand took Western Samoa away from Germany after World War I, and ruled it with the approval of the League of Nations.

Following World War II, the Samoans began to ask for self-government. In 1948, the two kings who shared leadership agreed on a design for a flag, which has been used since January 1, 1962, when the Independent State of Western Samoa (population 135,000) was established. Samoans say the red in their flag stands for courage, the white for purity and the blue for freedom. The Samoan language is used, along with English, by the government and in the schools.

150

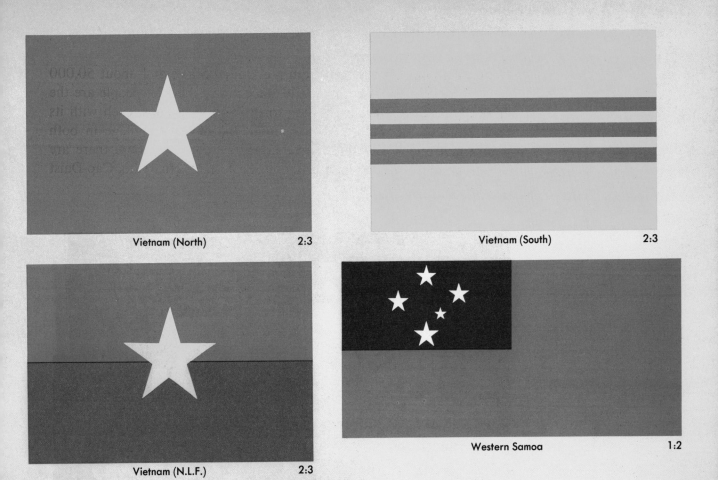

Vietnam (North)   2:3

Vietnam (South)   2:3

Vietnam (N.L.F.)   2:3

Western Samoa   1:2

YEMEN (YEM-un): In ancient times, Yemen was the wealthy kingdom of Saba, called Sheba in the Bible. The Sabaeans ruled much of southern Arabia and even crossed the Red Sea to rule in Ethiopia for a time. It may have been from Yemen that the Queen of Sheba went to visit King Solomon, bringing him gifts from her treasure of precious stones, spices and incense. Saba was a fertile land with more rainfall than other parts of the Arabian Peninsula, and its people were good farmers. About 650 B.C., the Sabaeans built an irrigation dam in the mountains, then used it for more than twelve hundred years. In A.D. 572, the dam broke and was never repaired, leaving the land it once irrigated dry and poor.

From the mid-nineteenth century on, the country was ruled by an *imam,* a Moslem religious leader who held absolute power, and its official name was the Moutawakkilite (meaning "Dependent on God") Kingdom of the Yemen. In 1962, rebels overthrew the imam and declared Yemen a republic. Fighting continued, with Saudia Arabia and Jordan helping the royalists, who wanted to put the imam back on the throne. The republicans were aided by the United Arab Republic.

The old flag of the kingdom was red, as are several other flags in

151

Arab lands, with a sword and five stars. The new flag of the Yemen Arab Republic is identical with that of the United Arab Republic, except that the Yemenite flag has only one star. The black stripe stands for the dark days when Yemen was ruled by the imam. The white stripe represents the ideals and purity of the revolution. The red is for the revolution itself. The 5,000,000 Yemenis speak Arabic, and almost all of them are Moslems. *Member, United Nations.*

YUGOSLAVIA (YOO-go-SLAHV-ee-uh): This country takes its name from tribes of people called Slavs who established the Kingdom of Old Serbia in southeastern Europe during the Middle Ages. In the fourteenth century, Serbia was invaded by Turks who ruled there for four hundred years. In 1804, when the Serbian people rebelled against the Turks, they used a flag of blue, white and red. This same color combination was also in their flag when they fought against Austria-Hungary in 1848.

At the end of World War I, an independent monarchy called the Kingdom of the Serbs, Croats, and Slovenes came into existence. The name was later changed to Yugoslavia, meaning "Land of the Southern Slavs," and its flag had the traditional blue, white and red colors.

When the armies of Nazi Germany occupied Yugoslavia during World War II, guerillas carried on a fight for freedom. Their flag was the tricolor of the Yugoslav monarchy, to which they added a five-pointed red star outlined in gold as a symbol of liberty and of the struggle for a new social order. After the war ended in 1945, the guerillas set up a government under communist leadership, and the guerillas' flag was made official. In 1963, the country adopted the name it now uses — the Socialist Federal Republic of Yugoslavia.

Eighty-eight per cent of the country's 20,000,000 people belong to five related Slavic nationalities, each of which is organized as a republic. Serbo-Croat (pronounced KRO-at) is the official language of the army of Yugoslavia and of the Serbs, Croats and Montenegrins. It is written in the Latin alphabet in one part of the country, and in another part it is written in Cyrillic letters, similar to those used for Russian. The Slovenes speak Slovenian and Macedonians speak Macedonian. All of these languages are used in schools, as are those of at least eight other small nationalities that make up 12 per cent of the population. Education is free in the schools and in the country's five universities. All religions are permitted. Among those who worship, about a third are Roman Catholics. Forty-two per cent are Eastern Orthodox, and 12 per cent are Moslems. *Member, United Nations.*

ZAMBIA (ZAM-be-uh): Missionaries from Scotland settled among the African people, along the Zambezi River, in the 1840's. Next came traders, gold miners, and finally, British troops. By the end of the nine-teenth century a large area north of the river had become part of the British empire and was known as Northern Rhodesia. In 1964, British rule ended, and the independent Republic of Zambia was established.

The 3,800,000 Zambians belong to 79 tribes, each tribe having its own language or dialect. Nearly half of the children under fifteen years of age are in schools, where the language they use is English.

The flying eagle in the flag symbolizes freedom and the ability of the country to rise above its problems. Red represents the struggle for freedom. Black stands for the people of Zambia. Green represents the rich countryside. Orange stands for mineral wealth. *Member, United Nations.*

UNITED NATIONS: In April, 1945, when preparations were being made for a conference in San Francisco that would establish the United Nations, some of the people who did the planning thought it would be appropriate for the organization to have a symbol. An agency of the United States government — the Presentation Branch of the Office of Strategic Services — was given the job of providing a design. The result was a map showing most of the world, with the North Pole at its center. In December, 1946, the General Assembly of the United Nations approved a slightly revised design that depicted the *whole* world, to indicate that the organization was meant to include every country. Two olive branches were added as a symbol of peace. The olive branch has stood for peace since the days of ancient Rome. On October 20, 1947, at its second session, the General Assembly adopted a flag that had this emblem in white on a blue field.

The blue and white flag flies wherever the United Nations conducts official activities and, of course, at the UN Headquarters in New York.

States gaining Independence, Feb., 1967 – Nov., 1968

ANGUILLA (ahn-GWEEL-uh): Island in the West Indies. Declared independence from the state of St. Christopher-Nevis-Anguilla *(see below),* May 30, 1967, and unsuccessfully sought membership in the Commonwealth of Nations.

ANTIGUA (ahn-TEE-gwah): Two islands in the West Indies. Became an independent member of the Commonwealth of Nations, February 27, 1967.

DOMINICA (dome-in-EEK-uh): Island in the West Indies. Became an independent member of the Commonwealth of Nations, March 1, 1967.

EQUATORIAL GUINEA (GHIN-ee): Between Cameroon and Gabon. Became a republic, independent of Spain, October 12, 1968. *Member, United Nations.*

GRENADA (gren-AID-uh): Island in the West Indies. Became an independent member of the Commonwealth of Nations, March 3, 1967.

MAURITIUS (maw-RISH-us): Island in the Indian Ocean east of Madagascar. Became an independent member of the Commonwealth of Nations, March, 1968. *Member, United Nations.*

Yemen (Royalist) 1:2

Yemen (Republic of) 2:3

Yugoslavia 1:2

Zambia 2:3

United Nations 2:3

Anguilla 1:2

NAURU (NOW-roo): Island in the central Pacific Ocean, formerly governed by Australia. Became independent, January 31, 1968.

ST. CHRISTOPHER [also called St. Kitts]-**NEVIS** (NEE-vis)-**ANGUILLA**: Islands in the West Indies. Together they became an independent unitary member of the Commonwealth of Nations, February 27, 1967. Although Anguilla later withdrew from the group, Britain still considers it part of the unitary state.

ST. LUCIA (loo-SEE-uh): Island near Barbados. Became an independent member of the Commonwealth of Nations, March 1, 1967.

SOUTHERN YEMEN (YEM-un): An area south of Yemen in the Arabian Peninsula. Official name is People's Republic of Southern Yemen. Became independent of British rule November 26, 1968. *Member, United Nations.*

SWAZILAND (SWAH-zee-land): Bounded by South Africa on three sides, with Portuguese East Africa to the east. Became an independent kingdom, September 6, 1968. *Member, United Nations.*

154

Antigua   2:3

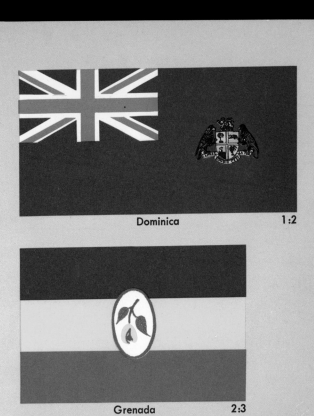

Dominica   1:2

Equatorial Guinea   1:2

Grenada   2:3

Mauritius   2:3

Nauru   1:2

St. Christopher-Nevis-Anguilla   1:2

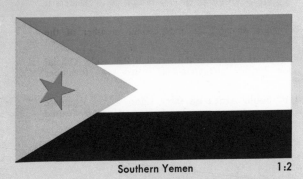

St. Lucia   13:21

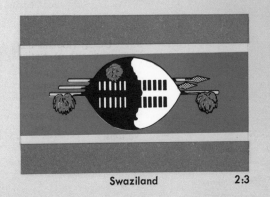

Southern Yemen   1:2

Swaziland   2:3

INDEX

Countries are listed under their popular names; full names of countries and correct appellations of their citizens appear in text of book. Italicized numerals indicate illustrations of national or state flags.

156

Castile

France

Sicily

Venice

China

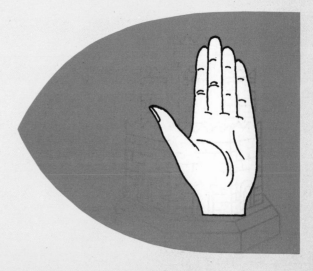

Sebastopol

Selected flags from "Book of the Knowledge of all the Kingdoms, Lords and Lordships